Creative Kids

Arts, Crafts & More

CRAYONS

MARKER

GLUE STICK

Written by
Barbara Lyerly Goins, Karen J. Goldfluss, Do[...]
Ina Massler Levin, and Patricia Miria[...]

Teacher Created Resources

Teacher Created Resources, Inc.
6421 Industry Way
Westminster, CA 92683
www.teachercreated.com

2004 Teacher Created Resources, Inc.

Reprinted, 2006

Made in the U.S.A.

ISBN #0-7439-3200-5

Editors:

Karen J. Goldfluss, M.S. Ed.

Gisela Lee

Illustrators

Howard Cheney

Sue Fullam

Keith Vasconcelles

Cover Artist

Brenda DiAntonis

The publisher and authors of this book have taken every reasonable precaution to ensure the users of this book that all activities and experiments are safe when directions are followed and done properly. However, the publisher and authors assume no liability from the conducting of these activities and experiments and further more advise parents, guardians, and/or teachers to supervise young children when attempting any of these activities or experiments.

Table of Contents

Table of Contents *(cont.)*

Table of Contents *(cont.)*

Introduction

The joy of creating and self-expression through art provides children with a very positive, active involvement in the learning process.

It is important to expose children to experiences in which they are allowed to connect their love of art with purposeful activities that can also be fun to create in school and at home.

We are faced with the ever-present challenge of a restricted budget, especially when it comes to art supplies. The purpose of this book is to provide children with activities that are inexpensive and accessible and to promote creativity and enhance learning as they make memorable projects.

This book is divided into nine sections.

Each section contains a variety of activities, many of which are multipurpose. Materials, directions, and suggested activities are listed for each project.

Suggestions for what materials to collect, how to store items to be used for crafts or art projects, and a list of easily recycled items from home or community are provided.

We know that you and your children will come away with many new, inexpensive, and creative ideas for using those materials you may have at one time considered discarding.

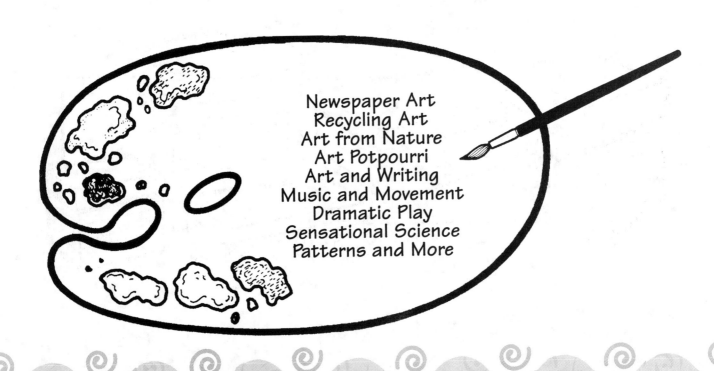

Newspaper Art
Recycling Art
Art from Nature
Art Potpourri
Art and Writing
Music and Movement
Dramatic Play
Sensational Science
Patterns and More

Recycle It!

Use any sturdy cardboard containers and boxes with lids to store materials for use throughout the year. The following boxes are easy to obtain and provide a variety of sizes and shapes from which to choose: grocery boxes, shoeboxes, stationery boxes, supply boxes, 10-ream copier paper boxes, and large ice cream containers.

Decorate boxes and lids according to what they contain.

- Use Christmas wrapping paper to decorate boxes that will contain Christmas cards.
- Use newspaper to decorate boxes that will contain old newspapers.
- Decorate a small box with any kind of paper and glue an item or picture on the end to indicate what the box contains. For example, put buttons on a decorated box to indicate that buttons are inside.

If you have available space, line up boxes on shelves so children can easily use them, either to add or take away supplies.

Set boxes on top of lids while materials inside are in use and then use the lids to close and store away materials until they are needed for the next project.

Collecting, Storing, and Recycling Materials *(cont.)*

Box It!

The following is a list of useful materials to have on hand for any of the projects in this book. Be sure that materials are properly stored in labeled boxes and accessible to parents, teachers, and children.

- newspapers and magazines
- used copier paper
- art tissue
- yarn, ribbon, string, thread, lace
- chenille sticks
- glitter, sequins, etc.
- buttons
- corn, beans, and seeds
- lids (plastic)
- paper goods
- juice cans
- seashells
- cotton swabs and cotton balls
- play money
- old crayons
- paper bags
- fabric bolts
- pretzels
- milk cartons
- plastic produce containers
- scraps of wrapping paper
- construction paper scraps
- cellophane
- pompons
- old keys

- old or used stamps
- wild flowers
- margarine tubs
- soda pop can tabs
- plastic forks and spoons
- small rocks
- toothpicks
- toilet paper/paper towel tubes
- doilies
- leftover icicles from Christmas tree
- round pizza boards
- craft sticks
- macaroni
- egg cartons
- stencils
- foam meat trays
- paper plates
- baby food jars
- bottle tops
- corks
- sponges
- rope
- coffee cans
- shoeboxes
- drawing paper
- sandpaper
- cardboard inserts
- beads
- shoelaces

- velcro
- fabric trim
- cotton batting
- empty spools
- buttons
- snaps
- zippers
- burlap
- felt
- leather
- old socks
- cotton fabric
- wool
- plastic fabric
- acorns
- pine cones
- dried flowers
- colored chalk
- old bed sheets
- wire hangers
- nails
- markers
- old toothbrushes
- marbles
- paintbrushes
- hole punch
- poster paint
- plastic bags
- wood cubes

Recycling Made Easy

An excellent way to introduce the idea of saving the environment while you are creating some spectacular art is to begin a recycling center of art materials you will use throughout the year. The following is a list of items and suggestions to help you get started. Give children a sense of purpose and ownership in the project by encouraging them to supply these and other materials. Brainstorm ideas for other recycled materials that may be used and their possible uses.

Soda Can Tabs

These can be strung together into chains for necklaces, hanging items, etc. Tabs also make wonderful additions to collages.

Juice Cans

Cover cans with yarn and glue labels or names on the outside. Decorated cans be used as gifts or as organizers.

Wood Cubes and Shavings

Use paint and markers to write numbers on cubes and use as dice. Use wood shavings to represent hair on art work, or glue shavings to collages to add texture.

Plastic Forks and Spoons

Make a bouquet or centerpiece of forks, spoons, and dried flowers. Tie them together with ribbon.

Make a stick puppet. With markers draw a face on a spoon. Add yarn for hair. Glue bits of cloth to the handle to make clothes.

Whatsits

Encourage children to create something new using one item from a recycle box you have made together.

Rocks

Start a collection of smooth, round rocks. Make rock creatures by adding eyes, legs, etc., using paint, markers, and recycled materials.

Margarine Tubs

These make excellent storage containers. They can also be used for science projects, planting seeds, water-related experiences, and sorting activities.

Placemats

Collect greeting cards, Christmas cards, etc. Arrange cards and glue them on construction paper. After the glue dries, laminate or use clear contact paper to protect the placemats.

Collecting, Storing, and Recycling Materials *(cont.)*

Paper Bags

Stuff paper bags with newspaper and tie them shut. Decorate bags to make characters from books, plays, etc., (see page 76) or design paper bag puppets (see page 75).

Toothpicks and Cotton Swabs

Use toothpicks to outline or create pictures. Cotton swabs can be glued to paper to make people and scenery. Glue toothpicks together to form toothpick sculptures.

Plastic Produce Containers

By weaving yarn into the sides of a one-pint (500 mL) produce container, children can make decorative gift containers.

Bottle Caps

Make 3-D grape or cherry clusters to use as decorative borders. Draw a pattern for clusters of grapes or cherries. Transfer pattern to heavy paper and cut out. Using felt (green or purple for grapes, red for cherries), draw circles to fit tips of bottle caps. Glue caps, face down, to the heavy paper.

Newspaper Dolls

Crumple newspaper into a ball to form the doll's head. For the body, roll newspaper into the shape desired. Roll and bend arms and legs as shown. Tape or tie body parts together. Paint and add features to the doll. Use yarn for hair.

Leaves

Collect an assortment of leaves. Trace on construction paper and draw veins. Do crayon rubbing by placing light-weight paper over leaves and rubbing a crayon back and forth across them. Cut out leaf shapes and laminate them for durability.

Homemade Art Supplies

Homemade Ink

This process is similar to one of the first ways writing ink was produced. The homemade ink can be used for writing activities and art projects. Homemade ink can be made from ripe blueberries or strawberries.

Gather the following materials: small jars with lids (baby food jars work well), a teaspoon or eye dropper, paper towels, paper cups, and some water.

Remove the stems and leaves from ripe berries. Place the berries in a small jar. Mixing different kinds of berries will produce different colored inks.

Press the berries to a pulp with the back of a spoon. When the berries are crushed, add water, one drop at a time, using a teaspoon or eye dropper. (The more water you add, the lighter the color the ink will be.) Stir the mixture well.

Place a sheet of paper towel over a paper cup. Push the paper towel down into the cup. Slowly pour the berry mixture through the towel pressed into the cup.

Let all the liquid drain through the towel. This is the slow part of the process. Remove the towel and throw it away. Pour the strained ink back into the jar. Use the jar as an ink container. The homemade ink can be used to write letters, poems, and stories. Dip a paintbrush in the ink and use it for a painting project.

Finger Paint

Gather the following materials: 1 cup (240 mL) water,
½ cup (120 mL) sugar, 1 tablespoon (15 mL) boric acid, 1 ¼ cups (300 mL) all-purpose flour, liquid cloves, food coloring, and a microwavable bowl or double boiler.

Boil 1 cup of water in the top of a double boiler or microwave. Add the mixture of sugar and flour and stir. Remove from heat.

Add boric acid and some liquid cloves to preserve the paint. Store the paint in an airtight container.

Colorful Pasta

Prepare various colors of macaroni ahead of time by soaking uncooked macaroni in food coloring diluted with water. (Adding a little rubbing alcohol helps the macaroni dry more quickly.) Use the colorful pasta for a variety of crafts or art projects.

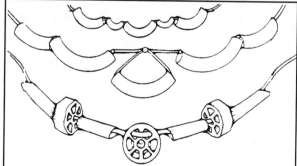

Watercolors

Make your own watercolors using the following ingredients: 1 teaspoon (5 mL) water; 1 tablespoon
(15 mL) vinegar; 2 tablespoons (30 mL) baking soda;
1 tablespoon (15 mL) corn starch; ½ teaspoon (2.5 mL) glycerin; food coloring. Mix vinegar and baking soda in a small cup or bowl. Add remaining ingredients and stir.

Inedible Dough

In a large saucepan, combine 1 cup (240 mL) flour,
1 cup (240 mL) water, 1 tablespoon (15 mL) salad oil,
2 teaspoons (10 mL) cream of tartar, ½ cup (120 mL) salt, and desired food coloring.

Stir the mixture constantly over medium heat, using a wooden spoon. When the dough begins to stick together enough to form a ball, remove it from the heat source but continue stirring. Place the hot ball of dough on a floured surface.

Knead the dough as it cools. The dough will be soft and pliable for molding into whatever shapes are needed for an art project.

You can make the dough in advance of an art activity and store it in the refrigerator. It also keeps well in a covered container in the freezer. Use the dough recipe for art projects throughout the year.

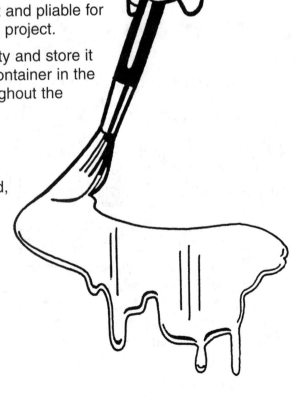

Play Dough

In a mixing bowl, knead 1 cup (240 mL) salt, 1 cup (240 mL) flour, and ½ cup (120 mL) water. If desired, add a few drops of food coloring to the dough. Store the play dough in a resealable plastic container or bag.

Bubble Solution

In a large container with lid, mix 1 gallon (about 4 L) of water, 1 cup (240 mL) liquid dish detergent, and 40–60 drops of glycerin. Stir well. Cover the container. Let the solution stand for about one week. (Aging the bubble solution allows it to produce thicker soap films.)

Bubble Wand

To make a bubble wand you will need a hanger, cotton string, pliers, scissors, electrical or duct tape. Prepare the bubble solution using the directions on this page. Bend the middle section of the wire hanger into a desired shape. Twist the end sections together to form a handle. To avoid sharp edges, cover the handle with tape.

Note to the parent or teacher: Create very large bubbles with two plastic drinking straws and a four foot (1.2 m) length of string. Pull the string through the straws and knot the ends. Place the bubble maker in the solution. As you gently lift the bubble maker out, spread the straws out to form a rectangular shape. Pass the bubble maker through the air to create huge bubbles.

Helpful Suggestions

1. Parents, family members, and teachers should become involved in the creative process and the activities.

2. Laminate children's art work.

3. Teachers can have samples from each child displayed at an open house. Let children share how they designed and assembled their projects. Similarly, parents and family members can have samples from their child displayed somewhere in the house.

4. Avoid the use of glass items, especially with small children.

5. Ask stores for their displays when they are finished.

6. Card companies will sometimes give you leftover cards and envelopes.

7. Obtain round pizza boards from pizza places.

8. Ask for empty fabric bolts from fabric stores.

9. Play classical background music as children work.

10. Read a related story or poem to introduce the activity.

11. Encourage creativity! While patterns are easy to use and attractive, they may limit a child's desire to explore and develop his or her own potential. Art should be fun, adventuresome, and, most of all, an expression of one's self!

12. For variety in texture and appearance, try some of these painting possibilities:
    - Paint by blowing through a straw.
    - Paint on a brown paper bag.
    - Paint on crumpled paper. (Crumple, open up, and paint.)
    - Sprinkle salt on paint.
    - Sprinkle glitter on paint.
    - Paint on corrugated cardboard.
    - Paint on fabric. (You might want to use fabric paint for this.)

Safety Guidelines

For Adults

1. Remember to read the directions completely and carefully before starting a project.

2. Actively assist with the crafts that need adult supervision for safety—those that require the use of an iron, stove, hot-glue gun, tools, sharp utensils, etc.

3. Thoroughly clean all previously used containers. Add a little chlorine bleach to the cleaning water to kill bacteria. Be sure to rinse out any chlorine residue and allow containers to dry thoroughly before use.

4. Never use meat trays that have held raw chicken. Egg shells should be rinsed inside and out with chlorine bleach to destroy potentially dangerous bacteria.

5. Cover work surfaces with a protective layer of cloth, plastic, cardboard, or newspaper.

6. Parcel out small items such as buttons and seeds one at a time to younger children. Be sure to stress that these items should never be put in their mouths.

7. Model "safety first" behavior as you work with your children. When you are through using a potentially dangerous implement, put it away, turn it off, or otherwise secure it to prevent injury.

8. Teach children to clean up and put things away in their proper places after completing the activity.

For Children

Be sure to ask an adult for help when you need to use any of the following items:

- sharp objects such as scissors, knives, pins, and needles

- hot items such as irons, hot-glue guns, and stoves

- tools such as hammers, screwdrivers, and sewing machines

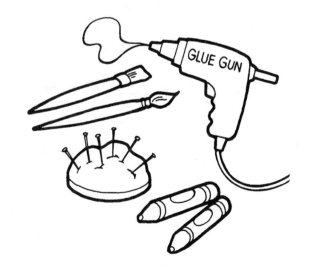

Newspaper Art

A Bounty of Bookmarks

Materials

- classified section of the newspaper
- scissors
- watercolors (Use a commercial product or prepare the homemade recipe on page 12.)
- paintbrushes
- construction paper or other heavy stock paper scraps
- glue
- optional: markers

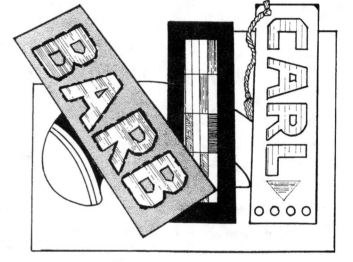

Directions

1. Cut a rectangle or other oblong shape from construction or heavy stock paper. Make the bookmark about 3" x 9" (8 cm x 23 cm).

2. Cut out a section from the classified ads of the newspaper. (This section produces the best geometric designs.) It should be smaller than the size of the bookmark. Decide what shape or design you would like to make on the bookmark. Children can personalize their bookmarks by cutting out letter shapes to represent their names or initials.

3. Watercolor the cutout newspaper design or outline blocks or color in sections of the newspaper ads with markers. Glue the completed newspaper section on the paper bookmark.

Extension

- Have children make bookmarks throughout the year. Keep an adequate supply of materials in a container so that children can make them at appropriate times during the day. Create both personalized and general bookmarks. These make wonderful gifts and reading incentives.

Peace

Materials

- newspaper
- pencil
- brightly-colored butcher paper
- scissors
- glue
- watercolors
- crayons or colored pencils
- paintbrushes
- ruler or large stencil letters (Letters are provided on pages 149–153.)

Directions

1. Place one of your hands (with fingers spread) on a piece of newspaper. Use a pencil to outline the hand. Children can help each other with this if necessary. Cut out the hand silhouettes.

2. Use the newspaper to draw and cut out letters for PEACE. You can make free-form letters if you wish or use prepared stencils. The letters will serve as a display title.

3. Color the letters using watercolors, crayons, or colored pencils. Glue letters to the top of a large piece of butcher paper.

4. Glue the cutout newspaper hands below the PEACE title. Arrange the hands to accommodate the activities you wish to present.

Extension

- Write stories, poems, or biographical information about famous peacemakers, Nobel Prize winners, ways to spread peace throughout the world, etc. Glue these on butcher paper and arrange the writings around the hand silhouettes.

Heart Art

Materials

- newspaper
- glue
- scissors
- two different colors of construction paper (one 9" x 12" or 23 cm x 30 cm piece of paper and one with smaller dimensions) per project

Directions

1. Cut an 8" x 10" (20 cm x 25 cm) section of newspaper.

2. Fold the newspaper sheet in half two or three times. You can fold along the length or width or a combination of both.

3. Cut heart shapes along the folds to produce a variety of hearts on the newspaper. Unfold the sheet of newspaper.

4. Glue the smaller piece of construction paper on top of the large one.

5. Glue the newspaper hearts sheet on the construction paper background.

Note: If the fold-and-cut method is too difficult for some children, have them draw and color hearts directly on the sheet of newspaper and then glue the sheet to the construction paper.

Extensions

- Use the heart to make Valentine's Day card covers for writing journals and/or "Special Moments" diaries.
- Heart art can also serve as a decorative background for bulletin boards displaying children's work.

Color Collages

Materials

- two different colored sheets of construction paper (one 8" or 20 cm square and one 7" or 18 cm square)
- one 6" (15 cm) square from newspaper ad section
- scissors
- glue
- watercolors
- paintbrushes

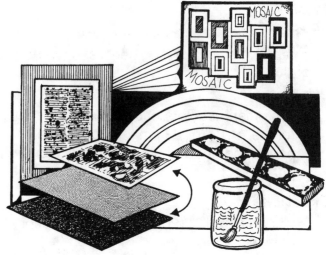

Directions

1. Watercolor here and there on a 6" (15 cm) square of newspaper that you have cut out. Be sure to leave some places white. Use a variety of colors. Allow the newspaper to dry.

2. Cut out construction paper and newspaper squares.

3. Glue the newspaper square on the 7" (18 cm) square of construction paper. Glue the 7" (18 cm) square of construction paper on the 8" (20 cm) piece.

Extensions

- Display the color collages on a wall using a mosaic pattern. To present a more striking mosaic pattern, use a variety of construction paper squares.
- Some children may want to drip glue and sprinkle glitter over the newspaper.

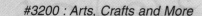

Patriotic Days

Materials

- newspaper ad or coupon section
- red and blue markers, pencils, or watercolors
- scissors
- glue
- one 9" x 12" (23 cm x 30 cm) sheet of white construction paper
- optional: small self-sticking stars

Directions

1. Cut out large blocks of ads or store coupons, approximately 7" x 9" (18 cm x 23 cm). If possible, try to choose pages of store coupons or ads that are similar in size.

2. Color the boxed areas on the ad/coupon block, alternating colors to create patches of red and blue.

3. Add self-sticking red and blue stars if desired.

4. Glue the newspaper on the white construction paper.

Note: When working on projects related to other countries, choose colors representative of those countries.

Extension

- Use black construction paper to make silhouettes of patriotic symbols or people. Glue them on top of the newspaper. Attach stories about patriotic symbols, historic events, and/or famous patriots. Display the art and writing activities.

Butterfly Silhouettes

Materials

- ad section of the newspaper about 7" (18 cm) square
- watercolors
- scissors
- glue
- one 9" (23 cm) square black construction paper
- paintbrushes
- optional: sequins or glitter

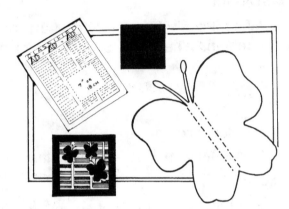

Directions

1. Cut out some newspaper ad squares.
   Watercolor blocks of ads. Use a variety of bright colors. If necessary, add a section of watercolor to make colors more vivid. Let dry.

2. Create a border by gluing the newspaper on the square piece of black construction paper.

3. Using black construction paper, draw and cut out silhouettes of butterflies.

4. Put glue down the center of the butterfly silhouettes and mount them on the newspaper ad. When dry, pull the wings up to give the silhouettes a three-dimensional look.

Note: Use other colors of construction paper for butterflies and mounting, if desired.

Extensions

- Add sequins or glitter to butterflies.
- Display the butterfly silhouettes when studying the life cycle of the butterfly.
- Replace the butterfly with silhouettes of other things from nature, such as flowers, birds, or frogs.
- Write haiku or other forms of poetry about your chosen silhouette.

Holiday Trees

Materials

- one 6" x 9" (15 cm x 23 cm) sheet of newspaper
- one 6" x 9" (15 cm x 23 cm) sheet of green construction paper
- glue
- hole punch
- magazines
- yarn or string
- scissors
- optional: glitter or sequins

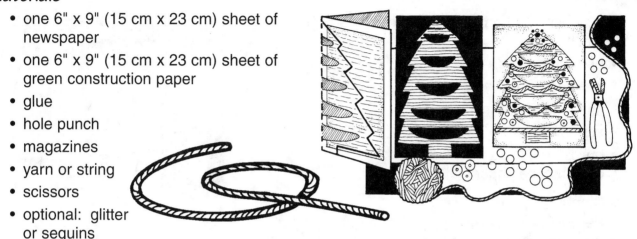

Directions

1. Fold the sheet of newspaper in half lengthwise. On the newspaper draw half of the tree outline so that the center of the tree is against the fold.

2. Cut out the tree outline with it still folded.

3. Cut out slices of the tree as shown below. (You can save these for making geometric designs and other decorations.)

4. Open the tree pattern and glue it on green construction paper.

5. Punch holes in colorful pages of a magazine. Make ornaments for the tree by gluing on punched-out circles. Trim the tree with yarn or string "garland." If desired, add glitter and/or sequins.

Extensions

- Make a holiday card by gluing a piece of construction paper on the back of the newspaper art. Write a holiday greeting on the inside.

- Use the basic newspaper tree pattern to make a forest background for bulletin boards, signs, and displays about the effects of deforestation and the need for recycling wood products.

My Own Menu

Materials

- school menu from newspaper or printed school menu
- pens or pencils
- watercolors or paints
- fine point black markers
- scissors
- one 9" x 12" (23 cm x 30 cm) sheet of construction paper
- glue
- paintbrushes
- optional: stencils letters (pages 149–154)

Directions

1. Cut out the school menu.

2. Use the fine point marker to draw some favorite foods on the menu. Watercolor the inside of the drawings.

3. Use stencils or hand-drawn letters to add a title at the top or sides of a sheet of construction paper.

4. Center and glue the menu on the construction paper.

Extensions

- Use seasonal construction paper such as orange/black for Halloween, red/green for Christmas, and red/white/blue for patriotic celebrations. Draw holiday foods on the menu.
- Cut out pictures of food from grocery ads and glue them on the menu.
- Cut out school or planning schedules and paint favorite subjects or activities on them. Mount the schedules on colorful construction paper.

24

Faces

Materials

- newspaper
- scissors
- markers
- construction paper
- glue

Directions

1. Draw a silhouette or a full-face outline of a face.

2. Mount the face on a piece of construction paper and use it for one of the extension activities.

Extensions

- If children have learned about some famous people, have them draw and cut out silhouettes of "faces in the news" and mount them on paper. Include a story or information about the famous person next to the silhouette.

- Younger children can draw a full-face outline. Add facial features. Glue the face on paper. Decorate it by adding yarn for hair, a hat made out of cloth and a real feather, etc. Have children give their faces a name and personality. Share the decorated faces with family and friends.

- Draw a silhouette of a character from a story or book. Add distinctive features to the character and have children describe why they chose this character.

3-D Trees

Materials

- watercolors or watercolor markers
- two 9" x 12" (23 cm x 30 cm) pieces of construction paper (green for tree, any color for frame)
- glue
- scissors
- classified ad section of the newspaper
- medium-point black markers
- paintbrushes

Directions

1. Cut a 7" x 10" (18 cm x 25 cm) rectangle from the newspaper ad section.

2. Color some blocks of ads using a variety of different colors.

3. Outline the colored blocks with a medium-point marker.

4. Glue the ad section to the center of the construction paper (frame).

5. Make a 3-D tree. Cut out a tree pattern (large irregular leaf section and a trunk section) and glue it to colored ads as shown.

6. Cut two smaller leaf sections and glue the center sections to the center of the tree pattern's leaf section. (When dry, fold these sections out to create a 3-D effect.)

7. Fold edges of construction paper (about 1" or 2.54 cm) toward the ad to make a frame. Pinch and glue the corners.

Extension

- Make 3-D frames for a variety of writing and other creative activities.

Dinosaurs

Materials

- white construction paper
- scissors
- newspaper
- glue
- pencil
- optional: dinosaur books or patterns, craft sticks, yarn, string, or a coat hanger

Directions

1. Draw a favorite dinosaur on white paper. Use pre-made patterns if necessary. Cut out the dinosaur pattern and use the pattern to trace the dinosaur onto newspaper.

2. Cut out the newspaper dinosaur and glue it to the white paper dinosaur. Allow the glue to dry.

Extensions

- On the white construction paper side, write the name of the dinosaur and some facts about it. Hang the dinosaurs in a room or make dinosaur mobiles on hangers.
- Younger children can make stick puppets by gluing the bottom of the dinosaurs to craft sticks.

Newspaper Fans

Materials

- newspapers cut into a rectangular shape
- scissors
- yarn or ribbon
- hole punch
- watercolors
- stapler or tape
- paintbrushes

Directions

1. Watercolor a newspaper rectangle. Allow the paint to dry. If children want to decorate the fans with glitter, sequins, etc., add these after the paint has dried.

2. Fold the newspaper into a fan shape.

3. With the fan closed, tape or staple one end of the folds.

4. Make a bow out of yarn and attach it to this end.

5. Punch a row of holes near the top of the fan and weave ribbon through the holes.

6. Tape the end pieces. (Weave a second row, if desired.)

Extension

- Make large newspaper fans. Write short "fan letters" to someone you admire from the past or present. Use paper that will adequately fit on an opened fan. Attach the letter to the front of the fan and display it on a wall or bulletin board.

Newspaper Trees

Materials

- four double sheets of newspaper
- scissors
- extra newspaper
- coffee cans or other containers

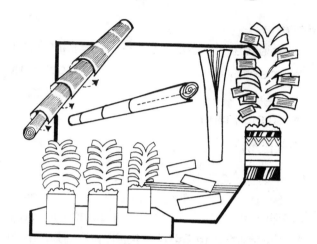

Directions

1. Spread out one sheet of newspaper and roll it up from the narrow end. Just before you reach the end, overlap another sheet to the end and continue rolling.

2. Continue the process until you have used all four pieces of newspaper.

3. Cut the top half of the roll in half. (See picture.) Then, cut the top in half again to split the top into fourths.

4. Hold the newspaper roll at the bottom and carefully pull the "branches" out from the top of the tree until it resembles the finished tree as shown on this page.

5. "Plant" your tree in the container using the extra paper to secure it.

Extensions

- Use a collection of trees to create a rainforest scene or cornstalks around a fall harvest or Thanksgiving display. Similarly, use a collection of trees to add a tropical look to a reading area.

- Make newspaper trees into word trees by attaching word cards to them. Words that fit a specific category can be placed on one tree with a label attached to the container identifying the category.

Accordion-Folded Newspaper Projects

Materials

- scissors
- newspaper
- markers
- stapler, glue, or tape
- index paper
- construction paper
- string
- *optional*: tongue depressors

Directions

Standard Accordion fold:

1. Spread a full-sized sheet of newspaper on a working surface. Cut two narrow strips (about 1½" or 4 cm wide) along the length of the newspaper.

2. Overlap two ends of each newspaper strip so that they are at right angles to each other. Staple, glue, or tape these two ends together.

3. Accordion-fold the strips for a pop-up card or "crawly." Lift the bottom strip and fold it over at the edge of the top strip. The strip which was on top is now on the bottom. Lift this bottom strip and fold it as you did the first one.

4. Continue folding the bottom strip over the top one until the strip is completely woven. Attach the end pieces.

Note: You can vary the width of the accordion-folded newspaper strips by changing the width of the strips. You can also attach several strips to make long, woven newspaper chains.

Extensions

Pop-up Cards

Fold a sheet of index paper in half. Decorate and/or write a greeting on the front cover. Glue small pictures, shapes, sayings, etc., to one end of the accordion-folded strips. (Use short strips for pop-up cards.) Glue the other end to the inside of a folded piece of index paper so that when it is opened, the card will pop up.

Marionettes

Choose a character for the marionette. Cut out a head and torso pattern. Use accordion-folded newspaper strips for the arms and legs; add hands and feet. Attach string to the hands, feet, and head. Crisscross two tongue depressors and tape them together at the center. Attach each piece of string from a limb to the end of one of the tongue depressors. Attach the string from the head to the center where the tongue depressors cross.

Nifty Names

Materials

- glue
- newspaper
- scissors
- construction paper
- homemade or commercial watercolors
- pens, pencils, or fine point markers
- paintbrush
- optional: fabric, glitter, sequins, buttons, shells

Directions

1. Using newspaper, measure and draw the letters of your name. (Younger children do better with tracing around precut letters. Letter patterns are provided on pages 149–153.)

2. Watercolor over the drawn letters. Let them dry. Cut out letters.

3. Glue the letters on construction paper in any arrangement.

Extensions

- Place finished names on fabric or other background and display them with children's writing.

- Decorate shoeboxes and glue your name to your box. Children can use the personalized boxes for supplies.

Creative Collages

Materials

(See individual activities below.)

Directions

Car Advertisements: Cut out car ads from the newspaper. Watercolor each and glue the ads onto a piece of construction paper or butcher paper.

Give the collage a title. Write your own car advertisements or use the collage to design ad posters for a new car dealership.

Older children can write some math problems involving car sales. Younger children can use the collages to identify similarities and differences among cars, car types, car parts, etc.

If different types of land transportation are used in a collage, classify them by number of wheels, vehicle use, etc.

"In the News" Collage:

Cut out newspaper articles relating to a specific subject or problem that you have learned about. Glue the collected articles on a large piece of paper in a collage fashion.

Add a title to the collage. Write related questions or main ideas for some of the articles in the collage.

Shapes Collage:

Draw geometric shapes on sheets of newspaper. Cut them out and glue them on paper. Label each shape.

Older children can add equations for finding the area, volume, or circumference of specific shapes. The collage can also be used as a visual reference. Younger children can use the collage for shape identification activities.

Face Collage:

Cut out pictures of faces from magazines and newspapers. Mount them on a large piece of paper. Include as many ethnic groups as possible, as well as young and old faces. Write stories to accompany the collage. Choose a theme such as "We are Family" or "The Human Family."

Newspaper Structures

For this project, children will be asked to make a structure out of newspaper. Working in small groups is an excellent way to foster creativity, and the added work force facilitates the assembly of the newspaper structures. Give children the freedom to choose the design of their structures.

Materials

- newspaper
- masking tape
- scissors
- string

Directions

1. Have children practice rolling newspaper sheets for the structures they will build.

2. Decide what kind of structure is going to be built and how the materials are going to be used.

3. Ask the groups to share their experiences with each other.

Extension

- Structures made from rolled newspaper are surprisingly strong. You can design specific structures such as bridges and towers and use them for a variety of activities.

Recycling Art

Paint Savers

Materials

- egg cartons
- markers
- several colors of tempera paint
- paintbrushes
- *optional:* fabric, glitter, sequins, buttons, shells

Directions

1. Collect egg cartons. Egg cartons can be used for art projects and games and as storage containers throughout the year so keep a supply on hand.

2. To use egg cartons for paint storage:

- Provide several cartons for easy access to paint as it is needed for art projects.
- Each child or group of children can have a paint carton. This makes distribution and preparation of materials for art projects much easier. Have children use markers to write their names on the lids. If possible, store the paint cartons in a cabinet or at an art center.
- For a painting activity, pour a different liquid tempera color in each cup. When children have finished painting, let the paint dry in the cup, close the lid, and set the carton aside.
- For the next paint activity, if paint remains in the cup, just add water and stir. If the cup is empty, put more of same color in the cup.

Extension

- Decorate an egg carton with yarn, fabric, beads, etc., and use it to store little keepsakes.

Paper Quilts

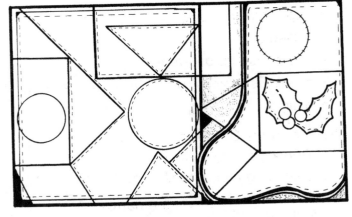

Materials

- pictures from old magazines
- scissors
- large pieces of cardboard or heavy paper
- glue
- markers

Directions

1. Select colorful pictures from old magazines.

2. Cut circles, squares, triangles, or other geometric figures out of cardboard or heavy paper for stencil patterns.

3. Use stencil patterns to cut out magazine pictures in geometric shapes.

4. On a large piece of cardboard, arrange shapes into a quilt pattern. Show children how to overlap the shapes.

5. Glue shapes to cardboard. Trim sides if any overlap.

6. With a marker draw tiny stitches to look as if it has been quilted.

Extensions

- Arrange pieces on a stocking pattern for Christmas. Add names, some holly with red berries, etc.
- Punch holes around the sides of each cardboard piece and "sew" several together with yarn for a large quilt.

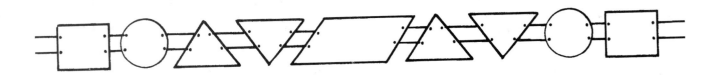

Bag Costumes

Materials

- large, brown grocery bags
- scissors
- string, belt, or yarn
- markers, crayons, paint, buttons, scrap material
- glue

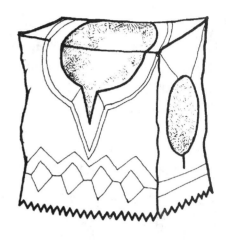

Directions for Costume Top:

1. Turn the bag upside down. Cut a circular opening on top for the head.

2. Cut out openings on the narrow sides of the bag (near head) for arms.

3. Decorate the grocery bag for the character portrayed. Use markers, paint, crayons, buttons, and any other scrap materials available.

Directions for Costume Bottom (Skirt):

1. Stand the large grocery bag upright.

2. Cut the bottom of the bag completely off to put the feet through.

3. Cut the skirt to the desired length.

4. Decorate for the character portrayed.

5. Gather the top of the skirt at the waist with a belt, string, or yarn.

Directions for Costume Bottom (Pants):

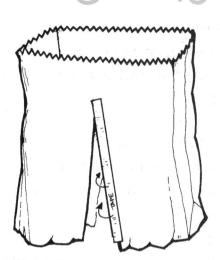

1. Stand the large grocery bag upright.
2. Cut the bottom of the bag completely off to put feet through.
3. Cut about halfway up each of the wide sides of the bag to form the legs. Tape along the inseam of the legs to close up.
4. Decorate for the character portrayed.
5. Put feet and legs in and carefully pull the pants up to the waist.
6. Use string, yarn, or a belt, to gather the bag around the waist.

Extension

- Use these bag costumes to put on plays, to depict favorite book characters, and for a variety of other activities throughout the year. You may wish to store some in boxes for spontaneous activities as well. They can be easily folded and stored.

The Ocean Blue

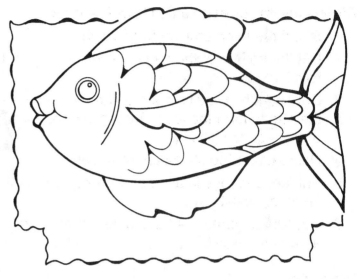

Materials

- white construction paper
- blue construction or butcher paper
- glue
- scissors
- crayons, markers, or watercolors
- colored magazine pictures
- plastic, bubble packing materials
- paintbrushes

Directions

1. On white paper, draw the pattern of a large fish.

2. Cut out the pattern and glue it on blue paper (ocean background).

3. Use crayons, markers, or watercolors to color the head, tail, and fins the same color.

4. Cut out scales from colored magazine pictures and glue on the fish.

5. With white crayon or chalk, make waves on blue water.

6. Put the bubble packing material over the pictures to create an underwater appearance.

Extension

- Make an underwater scene using a large sheet of blue butcher paper and add varieties of plants and sea life. Attach interesting fact cards about the plants and sea creatures.

Egg Carton Characters

Materials

- egg cartons
- chenille sticks
- material scraps
- sequins
- buttons
- markers or paints
- scissors
- glue, tape, or stapler

Directions

1. Cut the lid from the carton; save it to use later.

2. Cut out 12 cups from the egg carton. (You may not need all of them.)

3. Decide on the characters (people, animals, a character from a book).

4. Design the characters. Children can stack cups and add bits of carton, material scraps, chenille sticks, etc., to decorate their characters.

5. Use paint or markers to add features.

6. Set all characters on the lid to dry.

7. Share your egg carton characters with friends and family.

Extension

- Children can work in small groups to create characters they will use for a group display. They could recreate a scene from a story or write a new story about fictional characters they have created.

Crayon Art

Materials

- old crayons
- iron
- vegetable grater
- waxed paper
- old towel or piece of cloth
- newspaper
- construction paper
- containers

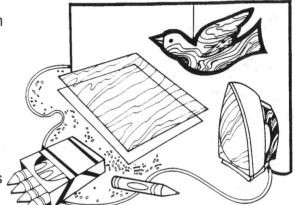

Directions

1. Place newspaper on a working surface. Collect an assortment of crayons that might otherwise be discarded. Separate the crayons into colors.

2. Use vegetable grater to shave the crayons. Collect the shavings by color in the containers.
   Note: Be careful with your fingers when using the grater.

3. Decide on a pattern in which to put the crayon art (e.g., a simple construction paper frame, a bird shape, or a flower shape). Cut out two patterns from a piece of construction paper so that the pattern becomes a frame.

4. Cut two sheets of waxed paper a little bigger than the dimensions of the pattern you will be using.

5. Place one piece of waxed paper on the covered working surface and sprinkle some crayon shavings on the waxed paper. (Do not overfill the waxed paper surface or sprinkle shavings too close to the edge.)

6. Place the other piece of waxed paper over the crayon shavings and cover them with a towel or cloth. Using a warm iron, melt the crayon shavings onto the sheets of waxed paper.

7. Use the pattern frame as a stencil and cut the waxed paper/crayon design to fit the frame. "Sandwich" the waxed paper design between the two frames and glue it in place.

Extension

- Display this colorful art by attaching thread or string to the tops of the creations and hanging them around the room or place them on windows for a stained glass effect.

Lacy Butterflies

Materials

- lace remnants
- scissors
- white thread or string
- chenille sticks

Directions

1. Cut out two lace rectangles, each about 2" x 5" (5 cm x 13 cm). Round the corners.

2. While holding the lace pieces horizontally, pinch the centers of each rectangle together to form the two sets of wings.

3. Wrap thread or string around the pinched center a few times and tie it tightly.

4. Bend a small pipe cleaner in half over the thread and shape it to look like antennae.

Extensions

- For variation, children can add sequins or use colored lace.
- Glue lace butterflies on the cover or inside of a thank-you or special-occasion card.
- Make gift boxes from sturdy boxes (with covers). Cover the boxes with wallpaper remnants. Attach one or two lacy butterflies to the top of the gift box.

Milk Carton Art

Materials

- small milk cartons
- newspaper, construction paper, wallpaper, or contact paper remnants
- scissors
- crayons, markers, or paint
- string or yarn
- glue or tape
- hole punch

Directions

1. Before starting a project, be sure that milk cartons have been cleaned and allowed to dry for a few days.
2. Open the carton along the top seam. Cover all surfaces with construction paper, wallpaper, or contact paper.
3. Have a theme when you design a carton. Place the title of the carton art on the top section of the carton. Cut out or draw pictures to represent the title on the sides and bottom of the carton.
4. Punch a hole in the center of the carton's top seam. Attach a piece of yarn or string to the carton and suspend it on a wire, a clothesline, or a hanger. Children can also keep their carton art in their rooms.

Extensions

- Write a five-verse or five-line poem using each side (surface) of the carton. Title the poem on the top portion of the carton.
- Flatten the top of the carton. Cover all surfaces with newspapers, wallpaper, material, contact paper, or construction paper. The covered cartons can be used as building blocks for many projects.
- Make a house from each carton. Choose a texture for the exterior, such as red or yellow construction paper for bricks, and another color for painted wood, etc. Draw bricks or wood and glue the textured exterior all around the milk carton. Add a roof and other exterior features. Assemble several houses into a town or village.

Decorated Pie Plates

Materials

- nail and hammer
- Styrofoam tray or heavy cardboard
- paper
- marker or pencil
- aluminum pie plate
- tape
- glue or glue gun

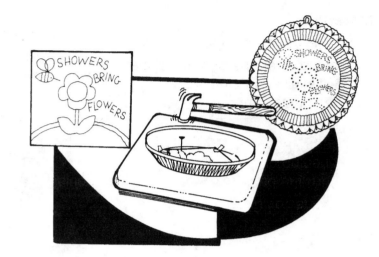

Directions

1. On construction paper, design a caption or illustration for your pie plate decorations.

2. Place the paper over the inside surface of the aluminum pie plate and secure it with tape.

3. Place the Styrofoam tray or cardboard on a work surface. Lay the pie plate on top of the Styrofoam tray. Use a hammer and nail to punch holes along the design lines on the paper and through the pie plate. The Styrofoam tray facilitates the hole punching and serves to protect the work surface. Remove the paper and enjoy your design!

Note: The use of hammer and nails should be supervised by an adult. Have younger children make simple designs or drawings on paper and then have an adult or older child punch the holes in the pie plate.

Extensions

- Decorate the pie plates by adding trim to the edge. Punch a hole at the top of the plate. Add string, yarn, or ribbon, and hang the decorated pie plate on a wall.
- Use decorated pie plates as gifts.
- Make them into plaques.
- Punch numbers, letters, or words on plates and use them for fun activities.

Reusable Tubes

Materials

- toilet paper or paper towel tubes
- a supply of one or more of the following—pictures from magazines, yarn, string, ribbon, newspaper, fabric remnants, construction paper, paint, markers, tissue paper
- glue
- tape
- scissors

Directions

Tube Mailers:

Decorate the outside of the tube with bits of colored magazine pictures or pieces of newspaper. Write a note, letter, or reminder on paper, roll it up, insert it in the tube mailers, and send it to a friend or family member. Have children make their own awards, place them in the decorated tubes, and present them to a special person.

Marble Run:

Have children work in groups to create a marble run using a series of tubes connected to form a kind of chute. Use masking tape to connect the tubes. Encourage children to design the most unique or fastest marble run they can. Have children share their marble runs and explain how they made their designs and the problems and/or successes they experienced.

Tube Treats:

Fill tubes with small gift items, treats, a small reward or certificate, etc. Cut a sheet of tissue paper about 5" (13 cm) longer than the length of the tube. Wrap the tube in tissue, leaving excess tissue on each side. Tie the ends of the tube with yarn, string, or ribbon.

Tube People:

Draw facial features on the tube. Paint or color the features and add yarn and other materials to complete the face. Place fingers inside the tubes and use as finger puppets. Make entire tube people figures by adding clothing and accessories. Tube people make interesting three-dimensional displays for bulletin boards.

Suggestions for Styrofoam

Materials
(See individual activities below.)

Directions

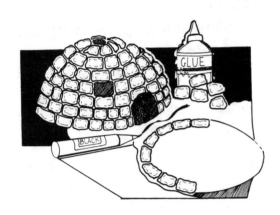

Igloos: Pour white Styrofoam packing material in a large open box. Draw a circle on a piece of cardboard. Glue white Styrofoam packing material around the circle line. Put glue on top of the first row of packing material and start another row. (Set this row in a little toward the middle.) Continue adding rows in this way until the pieces meet at the top in a dome shape. When the igloo is dry, use black marker and draw a door.

Note: Younger children will probably need assistance getting started with this project.

Styrofoam Letters, Designs, and Structures: Have children write letters or words on cardboard or heavy stock paper. Spread glue over the letters and press pieces of Styrofoam on the glue. Styrofoam letters can be used for bulletin board titles, children's names, and displays. Styrofoam can be cut into interesting three-dimensional designs. Create and paint Styrofoam designs or structures for a display.

Fast Food Boxes:
Collect sectioned Styrofoam boxes (with attached lids) from fast food restaurants. Try the following projects.

- Have children cut out pictures relating to a theme, area of interest, category, etc. Glue them in the sections of the fast food box. Make a title card and glue it to the cover. These can be displayed at a center for children to use.

- Collect objects that can be used for classification. Write a title and directions on an index card and attach it to the cover. Place items to be sorted in a plastic sealable bag.

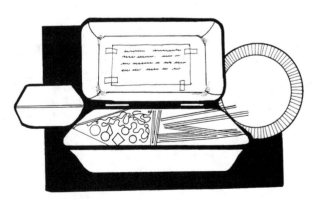

- Children can use the fast food boxes over and over again by changing the activity card and sorting objects.

Junk Boxes

Materials

- shoeboxes
- materials for decorating boxes—markers, paint, paper or material scraps, pictures, cutout letters, etc.
- scissors
- glue

Directions

1. Decorate the outside surfaces of the shoebox (including the lid). Children may want to personalize their junk boxes by adding their names. A set of letter stencils is provided on pages 149–154.

2. Fill the boxes with school supplies such as glue, rulers, paintbrushes, scissors, extra pencils, erasers, crayons, and resealable plastic bags (for small objects such as math manipulatives).

Extensions

- Decorate shoeboxes as a keepsake box to store your small treasures and mementos.
- Decorate shoeboxes and present them as gifts for friends or family members. Place gifts or cards inside the box.

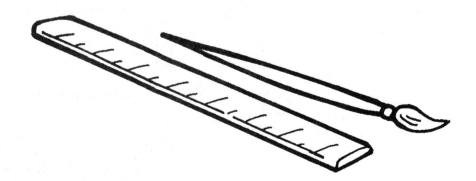

Patriotic Windsocks

Materials

- toilet tissue, paper towel, or wrapping paper tubes
- aluminum foil
- newspaper
- red, white, and blue watercolors, paints, or markers
- scissors
- string or yarn
- hole punch
- glue or tape

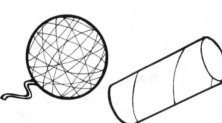

Directions

1. Use watercolors, paints, or markers to color tubes with red, white, and blue stripes or designs. Cut out star shapes from aluminum foil and glue them to the tube.

2. Make streamers by cutting 1" x 24" (about 3 cm x 60 cm) strips of newspaper and attaching them to the bottom end of the tube. Children can color or paint the strips.

3. Punch three or four holes near the top of the tube. Tie a piece of yarn or string to each hole. Bring the yarn or string up evenly and tie them together. Hang the windsocks near a window or doorway. If possible, take them outside and attach them to a tree.

Extension

- Make patriotic windsocks for Veteran's Day, Memorial Day, or the Fourth of July. Replace newspaper streamers with red, white, and blue paper streamers. Write the names of patriots or familiar patriotic expressions on the streamers.

Card Mobiles

Materials

- old or used greeting cards
- scissors
- construction paper
- yarn or string
- hangers
- hole punch

Directions

1. Cut out some pictures from greeting cards. The pictures should reflect a theme or topic which you will write a poem or story about.

2. Punch a hole at the top of each picture.

3. Tie string or yarn to the hole and attach the other end of the string to the hanger.

4. Cut a rectangular piece of construction paper to fit inside the hanger. On the paper write poems or short stories about the set of pictures you have chosen.

5. Punch holes in the corners of the construction paper. Tie yarn or string to the holes and attach the paper to the hanger. (**Note:** To use lined paper for writing, cut a rectangular piece of lined writing paper about the same size as the construction paper and write your poem or story on it. Glue the finished poem/story on the construction paper.)

Extensions

- Cut out a large assortment of pictures from greeting cards. Store them in a box. Hang several pieces of yarn from the hanger and attach a large paper clip to the end of each piece. Attach a blank sign for the center of the hanger using the directions in steps 4 and 5 above. Choose greeting card pictures that are related in some way to the hanging yarn or string. Clip them to the yarn/string.

- Use the mobile for a variety of activities in which children try to connect pictures to a title or activity they have written in the center of the hanger.

Shamrock Quilts

Materials

- various colors of construction paper (including green)
- scissors
- markers or crayons
- glue
- butcher paper

Directions

1. Fold and cut out three identical, large green hearts.

2. Draw a black line down the center of each heart.

3. Cut out a green stem.

4. Using markers or crayons, make a pattern or design on each heart. Be sure to make each half different than the other.

5. Glue the hearts together to make a shamrock. (See illustration.)

6. Glue your shamrocks to different color squares of construction paper. Make a quilt by gluing the shamrock squares in a quilt pattern to a large piece of butcher paper. With markers, draw stitches connecting the shamrock squares.

Extensions

- Use other materials such as fabric or wallpaper scraps to cover each half of the hearts.
- Change the shamrock into a flower by adding one or two more hearts to form the petals of the flower. Add a stem and leaves.

Egg Carton Wreaths

Materials

- paper plates
- egg cartons
- paintbrushes
- ribbon
- scissors
- tempera paints
- glue
- glitter

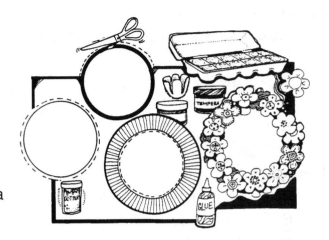

Directions

1. Cut the center circle from a paper plate (any size). Store the cutout circles for other art projects where you might need a circle shape.

2. Paint the ring green. Allow it to dry.

3. Cut off the lid of the egg carton.
   The lids can be used for storing materials such as scissors, pencils, and crayons, etc.

4. Cut out each of the cups in the egg carton. Carefully cut slits into the top of each cup and spread the slit sections out to form petals.

5. Dip the petals in tempera paint. (Choose flower colors.) Allow the petals to dry.

6. Glue the bottom of each egg carton flower on the paper plate ring until it is covered with flowers.

7. Put a drop of glue inside each flower and sprinkle some glitter in the center. Allow it to dry.

8. Add a colorful bow made from ribbon or construction paper.

Extensions

- Wreaths can be made as decorations for many occasions. Use the paper plate rings as the foundation for the wreath. For Christmas, cut green tissue into small strips. Twist each strip in the middle. Glue the twist to the ring. Fill the entire wreath with tissue twists. Add other holiday decorations and glitter.

- Display colorful wreaths around the room with children's work, illustrations, photos, etc., in the centers of the wreaths.

Store Simulations

Materials
- empty food boxes and cans
- grocery bags
- large paper scraps for signs, labels, etc.
- markers
- pencils
- play money
- *optional:* calculator

Directions
1. Be sure boxes, cans, cartons, etc., are clean. Check items for sharp edges.

2. Discuss about the tasks and materials that need to be considered when owning or managing a store.

3. Set up a store. Categorize the items and arrange them by section in your store.

4. Make signs, price labels, etc.

Extensions
- This is a wonderful way to learn about math or nutrition.
- Ask friends or family members to be clerks, cashiers, and customers. Alternate jobs so that each person has an opportunity to experience more than one role.
- Set up a checkout counter. Use play money. If possible, bring in a toy cash register and some calculators. As the cashier calculates the charges, the clerk bags the groceries.
- As an alternative to the grocery store, set up a clothing store. Use clothes that are intended for donations to a community organization or a school clothing drive. Price and purchase the items in the store. When finished, box the clothing for donation to a favorite organization.

Cake Mix $ 2.39

Tear Art

Materials

- glue
- paper
- pencils, markers, or crayons
- tagboard or cardboard
- scraps of art tissue, construction paper, newspaper, magazines
- *optional:* egg carton tops

Directions

1. Create a scene on a piece of tagboard or cardboard. (For this project it is suggested that scenes be simple and large areas so that children can glue torn pieces of paper.)

2. Tear pieces of art tissue paper, construction paper, newspaper, magazines, etc. Store them in an egg carton top, if available.

3. Glue the torn pieces to the tagboard or chalkboard. Choose an area of the scene—a grassy hill, for example—and glue torn green art tissue to it.

4. Glue another section with another color or a different kind of torn paper.

Extensions

- When the scene is complete, write stories or poems about them. Share the art and writing experiences with others.
- Create a card with a mosaic pattern or colorful collage and give it to a friend, family member, or teacher.

Box and Tube Castles

Materials

- cardboard boxes
- tape
- string knife
- glue
- paper towel tubes
- tempera paints
- scissors or craft
- paintbrush

Directions

1. Cut off the top of a box. Use the top to make a roof (step 6). All around the top of the box, cut evenly spaced slits about one-fourth of the way down. Push in every other set of slits to form the notched tops of the castle walls.

2. Make a drawbridge by cutting the sides and top of a door opening and leave the bottom of the door uncut.

3. Poke two holes in the wall above the drawbridge opening and two holes in the top corners of the drawbridge. Thread a piece of string through the opened drawbridge to the top holes in the wall and back through the other hole in the drawbridge. Knot the ends of the string.

4. Create towers from four paper towel tubes. Cut slits at one end of each tube and push in as in step 1.

5. Position the towers as shown below and glue the tubes to the castle. Allow the glue to dry.

6. To make a roof, tape or glue the box top on the folded-in tabs.

7. Cut out or paint windows. Paint the castle.

Extensions

- Have several groups make box-and-tube castles. Create a three-dimensional medieval scene complete with feudal villages.

- Use a box and tube castle as part of a center for books and stories about dragons, kings, knights, etc.

Computer Paper Edges

Form-feed computer paper edges can be used for a variety of activities. Collect and store a supply of paper edges to use throughout the year. If possible, obtain a variety of colors.

Materials

- dot matrix printer computer paper edges
- glue
- construction paper
- paint or markers when applicable

Directions

Use computer paper edges for the following projects:

- Make rings for decorative chains to be used at a party or other special occasion. Cut computer edges into shorter strips. Make a ring shape from one strip and glue the ends together. Slip another strip through the ring and glue its ends together. Continue until you reach a desired length. (Chain rings can be made the same size by counting a specific number of holes before cutting.)

- If possible, use a variety of colors for a more festive look. Make red and green chains for Christmas. Use red, white, and blue chains for patriotic holidays.

- Create a decorative frame for a picture, children's writing, etc. Have children leave space around the art or writing project.
  Make a frame by gluing a single or double frame of computer paper edges around the project being framed.

- Use the computer paper holes for a math lesson in counting groups of 5's, 10's, etc. Since the holes in standard dot matrix printer computer paper are $\frac{1}{2}$ inch (1.3 cm) apart, the paper edges can be used for standard measurement activities involving U.S. customary measurements. Younger children can also measure objects and make comparisons using the paper edges as a nonstandard measuring tool.

- Make pictures with computer paper edges. Draw an object or simple design on a piece of construction paper or cardboard. Glue paper edges over the line drawing. Color or paint the inside sections of the picture.

Bottle Terrariums

Materials

- two-liter plastic soda bottles
- metal spoons or butter knives
- craft knife
- aluminum foil
- small rocks or pebbles
- enriched soil
- plants
- water
- *optional:* insects

Directions

1. With a spoon or knife, carefully pry the bottle from its base.

2. Using a craft knife, cut off the bottom three inches (8 cm) from the bottle. Set the plastic bottle aside.

3. Line the bottom and sides of the base with foil. Place a few small rocks or pebbles inside the container. Half-fill the container with soil. Set plants in soil and continue to fill the base with soil until the soil level reaches about one inch (about 3 cm) below the rim.

4. Add insects and/or decorative rocks or twigs. Water soil until moist.

5. Cover the soil section with the plastic bottle, fitting its bottom edge inside the rim of the soil section. Re-cap the bottle tightly. (If a cap is not available, cover the bottle with a small piece of foil.)

6. Place the terrarium in a sunny area but not in direct sunlight. Add a few drops of water periodically if the soil seems to be getting dry.

Extensions

- Use the terrarium to study plant and animal life.
- Keep a daily or weekly journal of what happens in your terranium.

Santa's Reindeer

Materials

- glue
- tape
- tall plastic, cardboard, or metal cans (with lids)
- brown construction paper
- scissors
- measuring tape
- red, white, and green felt scraps (Substitute with construction paper if necessary.)

Directions

1. Cover the can with brown construction paper. Tape or glue the edges together.
2. To make antlers, trace your hands on brown construction paper. Make two antlers.
3. Draw and cut two brown paper ears. Cut two small white felt ears and glue them inside the brown ears.
4. For the head, cut brown strips of paper 3" (8 cm) wide and 14" (36 cm) long. Fold them in half. Trim the two corners opposite the fold by making a 45 degree cut. Glue the head near the top of the can. (The fold should be just under the lid, and the flap should hang loose.)
5. Draw two white oval eyes on white paper. Color the pupils black. Glue the eyes on the head flap.
6. Cut a large round nose from red felt and glue it under the eyes.
7. Glue an ear on each side of the face; glue the antlers behind the ears.
8. Cut holly from green felt, berries from red felt, and a bell from white felt. Glue these along the bottom of the can.

Hint: Felt may be too hard for younger children to cut. Have an older friend or family member assist with the cutting.

Spool Prints

Materials

- large, empty thread spools
- pencils, thin wooden dowels, or knitting needles (Choose an item with a diameter that will allow it to fit through the center hole of the spool.)
- non-hardening clay
- craft sticks or sharpened pencils
- old baking trays or Styrofoam trays
- construction paper or index paper cut to desired size
- tempera paints
- scissors
- soap, water, and paper towels for cleanup

Directions

1. Prepare rollers by first covering the surface of the empty spool with about ½" (about 1.5 cm) layer of clay. Smooth the surface of the clay as much as possible and check to see if the clay is approximately the same thickness all around.
2. Push the pencil, wooden dowel, or knitting needle through the center hole in the spool.
3. Make patterns on the roller by pressing designs into the clay with a sharpened pencil or a craft stick. (For finer impressions use the end of a paper clip.)
4. Pour tempera paints into the baking tray or Styrofoam tray. Hold the ends of the spool roller and roll it back and forth across the paint until the entire clay surface of the roller is covered with paint. The roller is ready to use.

Extension

- Create a design on paper by pushing the roller across the paper in the area where you want the design to appear. Spool prints can be used to border welcome cards, bulletin boards, or children's work. To use more than one print color on a piece of paper, wash the paint off the roller with soap and water and pat it dry with a paper towel before each new color is added. Wait until one paint is dry before adding another.

Art from Nature

Mushroom Prints

Materials

- ripe, store-bought mushrooms (If possible, use mushrooms with large caps.)
- white paper
- plastic cups or containers

Directions

1. Rinse and clean the mushrooms.

2. Look closely at the "wheel spokes" pattern on the underside of the mushroom caps. This pattern is produced by the gills. Carefully break off the stem of the mushroom.

3. With the gill side down, place the mushroom on a white piece of paper and cover it and the paper with the cup/container. Leave the mushroom cap covered for about three hours.

4. Gently lift the cup or container off the paper. Remove the mushroom cap and observe what has happened—the spores which have fallen from the gills produced a "wheel spokes" pattern.

Extension

- Children enjoy making these spore prints and will probably want to make more. Invite them to make their spore print patterns into a work of art.

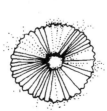 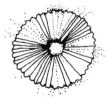 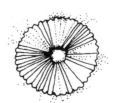 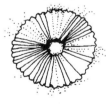 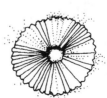

Pressed Wild Flowers

Materials

- glue
- nonpoisonous wild flowers
- bright colored construction paper
- colored cellophane paper
- scissors
- black construction paper

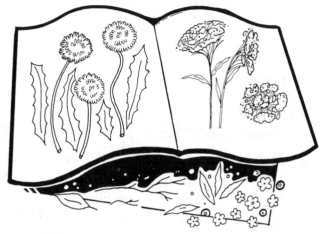

Directions

1. Gather nonpoisonous wild flowers. (Queen Anne's lace is excellent.)

2. Press flowers between book pages for several days.

3. Remove the flowers from the book; carefully cut them to an appropriate size and glue the flowers on a piece of brightly colored construction paper. Allow the glue to dry.

4. Cover the entire piece of construction paper with a sheet of cellophane paper and glue the edges of both pieces of paper together.

5. Make a frame from black construction paper and glue it to the cellophane.

Extensions

- For a three-dimensional effect, replace the pressed flowers with twigs, leaves, and grass. Do not add the cellophane covering. Frame the pictures as in step 5.

- Display framed wild flowers around the room or on windows. Write about the flowers or how you picked and assembled the framed flowers. Write haiku or other poetry about nature.

Dried Flower Arrangements

Materials

- wild flowers or other fresh-cut flowers
- nails, wire, string, or coat hangers
- scissors

Directions

1. Cut the flower just before they are in full bloom and remove the leaves.

2. Group flower families together by using a string or rubber band to tie their stems together. Be sure not to smash the blossoms tightly together because air must be able to circulate around the petals to thoroughly dry the blossoms in their original shape.

3. In a warm, dry, clean, airy, dark place, hang the flower groupings upside-down, suspended from a nail, wire, string, or coat hanger. They will dry in three to five weeks.

Extensions

- Dried flowers arrangements can be used to decorate tables at school and at home.
- Make a bouquet by arranging a variety of dried flowers, tying them together, and adding a decorative ribbon. Create dried flower bouquets as gifts.

Cornhusk Dolls

Materials

- string or yellow yarn
- paper towels
- cornhusks (available in grocery stores in Mexican food sections)
- bucket or pan for soaking cornhusks

- *optional:* fabric or yarn
- cotton
- water
- paints
- scissors
- cloth or sponge

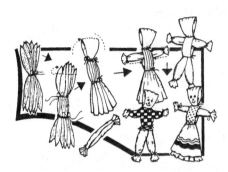

Directions

1. The husk is the foliage of the corn or maize plant that wraps the ear tightly in a protective coat. Cornhusks are tough. They can be braided, wrapped, twisted, and knotted.

   Prepare the husks by soaking them in warm water until they are soft (up to one hour). Drain husks on paper towels. Keep the husks damp with a cloth or sponge while working with them.

2. Put six cornhusks together and tie a string around the middle for the doll's waist. Tie another piece of string about 2" (5 cm) below the first to form the body. Fold the ends of the husks down from the top and hold them down by tying them in place with another string placed on top of the first string that was tied in the middle.

3. To form the arms and hands, put two husks together and tie them near the ends with strings. Roll and slip the arms through the opening in the top of the body near the neck or tie the arms to the body by wrapping string around them at the neck.

4. For a skirt, keep the bottom of the dress as is. To make pants, divide or cut the husks below the waist. To form the legs and feet, roll the divided husks into trouser legs and tie them with string near the bottom.

5. Paint a face and clothing on the doll. If scraps of fabric are available, sew or glue them on the doll. Add hair by gluing paper strips, cotton, yarn, or fabric to the head.

Extension

- Use cornhusk dolls for autumn displays.

Pine Cones for the Holidays

Pine cones can be used in the making of projects or as part of the materials used for preparing art projects.

Materials

(See individual activities below.)

Directions

Christmas Pine Cones: String out bits of cotton on pine cones. Sprinkle them with silver glitter.

Use the decorated pine cones for a table centerpiece or to create a winter scene. Make pine cone wreaths and decorate them with holiday ribbon and ornaments.

Thanksgiving Turkeys: Use a large pine cone for the body of the turkey. Add feathers (real or cut from construction paper) by gluing them in a circle to the base of the pine cone.

To make the head, dip a Styrofoam ball into brown paint and allow it to dry. Glue the ball to the other end of the pine cone. Cut two eyes, a mouth, and a nose from flannel scraps and glue them on the head. Cut a section of a red chenille stick and glue it on the head. (Color a white chenille stick with a red marker, if a red chenille stick is unavailable.) Shape chenille sticks for feet.

Holiday Candles: To make candles and a holder you will need to collect the following: small round-shaped pine cones, toilet tissue tubes, and small foil pans. Cover a toilet tissue tube with red, green, silver, or gold paper. Put glue in the bottom of a foil pan.

Place the toilet tissue tube in the center of the pan. Arrange pine cones around the base of the tube. Fill the tube with newspaper until it is stuffed. Cut a flame shape from construction paper and glue it to the top of the tube. Sprinkle glitter (silver or gold) on pine cones or add tiny red or green ribbons, if desired.

Plant Rubbing Collages

Materials

- glue
- flowers, leaves, grass, or bark
- lightweight white paper (not construction paper)
- crayons
- newspaper
- construction paper (any color)

Directions

1. Collect a variety of leaves, grasses, tree bark, woody stems, and flowers.

2. Cover the working surface with newspaper to make cleanup easier.

3. Choose a plant for the first rubbing and cover it with a piece of lightweight white paper.

4. Using a crayon, rub over the surface of the paper that covers the plant. (For best results, have children rub the crayon on its side.)

5. Cut out the design made by the plant rubbing and glue it on construction paper.

6. Choose another plant from the assortment and follow steps 3 through 5. Continue mounting plant rubbings until the collage is complete.

Extensions

- Use the activity to teach the different kinds of leaves, flowers, etc.
- Make autumn leaves by using orange, green, yellow, red, and brown crayons.
- Replace crayons with pencils to create an outline of the plant and color the plant parts with watercolors.

Pussy Willow Displays

Materials

- glue
- pussy willows (found in most floral shops)
- construction paper or index paper
- markers
- watercolors, crayons, or colorful tissue paper scraps
- stapler

Vases of
pussy willows

All in the air

Beautiful pictures
Looking so fair.

Susie

Directions

1. Make a vase for the pussy willows. Decorate one side of a 9" x 12" (23 cm x 30 cm) piece of construction paper or index paper. Draw designs on the paper or glue tissue paper scraps in a collage design.

2. To make the vase, hold the paper lengthwise and form a cone shape. Glue the seams together.

3. Staple the vases to a large bulletin board or poster board.

4. Arrange some pussy willows in the vase. Allow some pussy willows to extend from the sides and top of each vase.

Extension

- On a large bulletin board or poster board, arrange a display of your poems, stories, etc., around the vase.

Egg Carton Gardens

Materials

- cattails (or any wild flowers with a stem)
- egg cartons
- glue
- scissors
- green paint
- green construction paper
- pencil

Directions

1. Remove the egg carton lid. Cut the cup section in half.
2. Turn the carton half upside down (cups facing down).
3. Paint the upside down carton green.
4. Make a thin strip of grass from green construction paper to cover all sides at the base of the carton.
5. Glue the grass around the bottom of the carton.
6. With a pencil, punch a hole in the top of each egg carton cup and insert cattails.
7. Cut out petal shapes from the leftover egg carton cups. Use the petals to make little flowers.
8. Decorate the flowers with green leaves (cut from construction paper) and glue them inside the grass border near the bottom of the cattails.

Extensions

- Use flower arrangements as centerpieces for special celebrations or activities.
- Make flower arrangements as a gift for a friend, relative, or teacher.

Autumn Centerpieces

Materials

- acorns
- red, green, yellow, orange, and brown construction paper
- pencils and black markers
- large plastic lid or round piece of cardboard
- glue
- scissors
- *optional:* baby's breath

Directions

1. On construction paper, trace one of your hands (and part of the arm) to create a leaf pattern. Use a variety of fall colors to make the patterns.

2. Cut out the patterns and draw leaf veins with a marker.

3. Using a plastic lid or cardboard, arrange leaves along the perimeter, leaving an opening in the center. (Use the arm section of the pattern as a tab. Turn it under and glue it to the lid or cardboard base.) The hand pattern leaves should stand up.

4. Arrange acorns in the center of the circular pattern of leaves.

5. Fill in areas of the acorn center with baby's breath.

Extensions

- Make centerpieces with holiday themes. For example, in a Thanksgiving centerpiece, people can write about what they are thankful for and add straw, gourds, miniature pumpkins, etc., for decoration.
- Make Attention Getters as on page 81 with a fall theme or phrase.

Leaf Printing

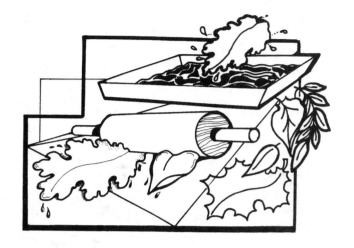

Materials

- a variety of leaves
- tempera paints
- large foil pan or tray
- newspaper
- construction paper
- soap, water, and paper towels (for cleanup)
- *optional:* rolling pin and waxed paper

Directions

1. Cover work surface with newspaper.

2. Pour liquid tempera paint into a large foil pan or tray.

3. Carefully lay a leaf on the surface of the paint.

4. Lift the leaf out of the paint and let the excess paint drip off.

5. With the paint side facing down, press the leaf on a piece of construction paper. (For a clearer print, place waxed paper on top of the leaf and move a rolling pin back and forth across the waxed paper.)

6. When the leaf print dries, cut out the pattern.

Extension

- Use a variety of paints and leaf designs. Make several leaf prints. Cut out the prints and mount each on a separate piece of paper. Add information about the type of leaf/tree represented on each page. Make an individual leaf book or combine your pages with those of your friends or family members.

Art Potpourri

Around the Kitchen

Materials

- kitchen utensils (no sharp objects)
- light-colored construction paper
- pencils, markers, or crayons
- tempera paint or watercolor paints
- scissors

Directions

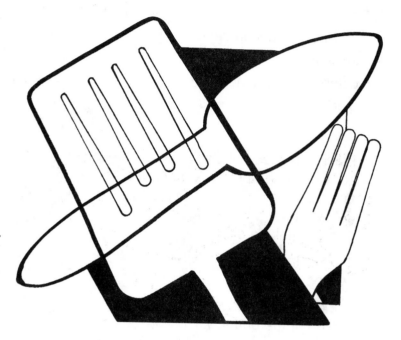

1. Gather some kitchen utensils and discuss the function of each.

2. Place a variety of utensils on construction paper.

3. Using a pencil, a marker, or a crayon, trace around each item to make an outline of each utensil. (Overlap utensils.)

4. Paint your kitchen utensil design with tempera or watercolor paints. (Substitute paints with crayons, if desired.)

Extensions

- Cut out the drawings/tracings of kitchen utensils and mount them on paper.
- Cut strips of butcher paper. Design and color a collage of kitchen utensils. Use the strips as a border for a poster on food or healthy eating habits.

Cellophane Butterflies

Materials

- black construction paper
- scissors
- colored cellophane
- glue or stapler

Directions

1. Place one piece of black construction paper on top of another and draw an outline of a butterfly. (For younger children, an adult may want to make a stencil first.)

2. Cut out the inside of each wing section, as shown.

3. Cut cellophane paper to cover the outline of the butterfly.

4. Glue the cellophane between the two black butterfly outlines.

5. Trim away excess cellophane.

6. To decorate the transparent part of the wings, add small pieces of construction paper or sequins to the cellophane.

Extensions

- Decorate windows or make a wall display to celebrate spring.
- Hang butterflies from the ceiling.
- Use cellophane butterflies for a science display or center or for a poetry unit on insects.

Tissue Paper Flowers

Materials

- one 9" x 12" (23 cm x 30 cm) sheet of white construction paper
- green watercolors or markers
- glue, tape, or stapler
- scissors
- pencil
- colored tissue paper
- ruler or meter stick

Directions

1. On the white construction paper, draw an outline of a few flowers complete with stems and leaves. Use a ruler or meter stick to measure a 1" (2.54 cm) border around the paper.

2. With green watercolors or markers, color stems and leaves.

3. Cut colored tissue paper into circles about the size of a half dollar. The circles will serve as petals for each flower. Make five or six circles for each flower.

4. To form a petal, evenly cover the end of a pencil with a circle and pull up around the pencil.

5. Dip the tissue circle at the pencil end lightly in glue and place the petal on the flower drawing.

6. Continue making and gluing petals until all petals are covered.

7. Make the 3-D frame by folding in the construction paper 1" (2.54 cm) along the edges. Tape, staple, or glue the corners together.

Extension

- Make flowers using the petal-making process described above and attach them to border displays and bulletin boards with spring themes.

Popcorn Trees

Materials

- black construction paper
- any other color construction paper
- scissors
- glue
- popped popcorn

Directions

1. On black construction paper, take turns tracing around your hands and those of a friend or relative to form trees. (White pencil or chalk works well for tracing.)

2. Cut out a tree pattern. Glue the tree on any color construction paper.

3. Glue popcorn to the tree. (Use colored popcorn if available.)

4. You may eat any left over popcorn.

Extensions

- Replace paper trees with twigs or small branches.
- Write popcorn poems or tell the "Story of Popcorn" on index cards and display them along with the popcorn trees.

Paper Bag Puppets

Materials

- paper lunch bags
- markers, crayons, or paints
- scissors
- glue

Directions

1. Make a face and other body parts for the puppet character. Be sure the parts are in proportion to the size of the bag. The face should be as large as, or a little larger than the bottom of the bag; the torso should fit on the front or back of the bag.

2. Cut out and decorate the puppet pieces.

3. Turn the bag upside down so that the bottom of the bag faces up. Do not open the bag.

4. Glue the head piece on the bottom flap.

5. Glue the torso of the puppet onto the flat, rectangular part of the bag just below the lower part of the head piece.

6. If the puppet has separate arms, glue them to the left and right of the character on the narrow, rectangular sides of the bag.

7. Place your hand inside the bag to make the puppet talk and move.

Extension

- Create new characters or make characters based on familiar stories or fairy tales. Make a puppet show stage using a large box. Prepare puppet shows using the paper bag puppets.

Stuffed Bag Characters

Materials

- glue or tape
- white or brown paper lunch bags (You will need three bags per character.)
- newspaper
- string
- markers, crayons, or paints
- scissors

Directions

1. Tear newspaper into strips. The strips are used for stuffing the bag.

2. Stuff one of the bags with newspaper.

3. Lay a paper bag flat on a surface with the opening at the bottom. Draw the body of the character on the side facing up.

4. Slide the bag with the body sketch over the stuffed bag. Glue the bags together or tie them together in the middle with string.

5. Turn another closed bag upside down and draw a face. Leave about three inches (8 cm) of room at the opening to tie the bag. Stuff the bag with newspaper and tie it with string.

6. Glue or tape the head onto the body.

7. If desired, add arms and legs. (For directions on how to make accordion folds, see page 30.)

Extensions

- Make stuffed bag characters to represent fictional characters from books the children are reading.
- Use stuffed bag characters for holiday or special occasion displays.
- Have children make stuffed bag characters of themselves. Use the characters as part of a representation of written work or projects.

Treasure Boxes

Materials

- a variety of uncooked pastas
- Colorful Pasta recipe (page 11)
- glue
- cigar boxes or shoeboxes (with tops)

Directions

1. Gather a variety of pastas—shells, elbow macaroni, bow ties, etc. Store each type in its own container.

2. Color pasta using the directions on page 11.

3. Have children glue pasta on the sides and top of the shoebox or cigar box. (To create an attached top for a shoebox, tape an edge to the box or slit the corners on one side of the top and glue the separated edge to the shoebox.)

4. Cover the entire surface with pasta or cover only the top with pasta and the sides with wallpaper, fabric, or construction paper.

Extensions

- Use the decorated boxes as gifts or to store special items, notes, materials, etc.
- Make a family or classroom treasure box. Store important materials in the treasure boxes.

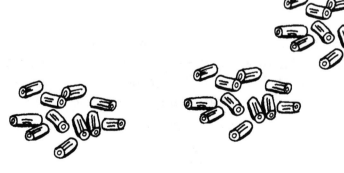

String Art

Materials

- string or yarn
- construction paper
- hole punch
- markers

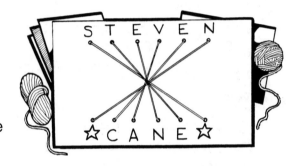

Directions

1. Print your first name in capital letters across the top of a piece of construction paper near the edge.

2. Punch a hole below each letter.

3. Print your last name in capital letters across the bottom of the paper near the edge.

4. Punch a hole above each letter.

5. Attach string or yarn from the holes at the top of the paper to holes at the bottom as illustrated below.

6. Thread a length of yarn or string back and forth through the holes by beginning at the top left corner and finishing at the bottom left corner. (Be sure to make a knot in the back of the first hole to secure the yarn.)

7. If your first and last names do not have the same number of letters, add stars, hearts, or a small illustration on either end of the shorter name so that the number of letters on the top and bottom of the paper will match.

Extensions

- Make string art pictures for matching facts or for problem-solving activities.
- Collect rectangular pieces of thin cardboard such as sketchpad or writing pad backings. Punch one or two rows of holes along the border of the cardboard and weave colorful yarn or string through the holes to create a frame. Children can use these to frame pictures, stories, poems, etc.

Napkin Art

Materials

- paper napkins or paper towels
- food coloring
- water
- bowls
- newspaper

Directions

1. Cover the work surface with newspaper.

2. Prepare bowls of different food colorings by adding a small amount of water and a few drops of food coloring to each bowl. You will enjoy mixing colors, such as red and blue to make purple.

3. Fold the napkin or paper towel in half and then in half again. Keep folding until it is small.

4. Dip each corner of the napkin or paper towel in food coloring.

5. Unfold the napkin or paper towel and allow it to dry on the newspaper.

Extension

- Make "gift-giver" napkins. Fold the napkin back into its original shape. (Fold the paper towel in half and then in half again.) Accordion-fold the napkin or paper towel and pinch it in the middle. Tie a piece of yarn or ribbon in the center. Spread the ends out to create a fan shape on each side. Slip a small gift through the yarn at the center of the napkin.

  Gift suggestions: pencil; candy cane or lollipop; poem, gift certificate, special coupon, or award rolled up like a scroll.

Tissue Paper Collages

Materials

- newspaper
- a variety of colored art tissue paper
- paintbrushes of various widths
- containers of thinned white glue or laundry starch
- scissors
- pencils or markers for sketches
- white or light-colored construction paper for background

Directions

1. Cover the work area with newspaper.

2. Begin by tearing a few small pieces of tissue of different colors.

3. Overlap the tissues on a small piece of white construction paper. (For best results, place dark colors on top of light colors.)

4. Brush the top surface with starch. The liquid penetrates the thin paper, blends the colors, and bonds the tissue to the background sheet.

    Hints: The brush may pick up color from the tissue and spread it to the background paper. This can become part of the design or can be avoided by stopping the brush before it reaches the background paper. Subtle shadings can be obtained by overlapping pieces of the same tissue color. Brilliant combinations and contrasts appear when different colors overlap.

5. Let the tissue dry thoroughly before adding details and textures. Add subject matter by sketching an outline or make planned shapes without one. Fill in the outline with tissue. (Tissue can be cut to a sharp edge, torn for a softer look, or added in small pieces to fill in an outline.)

Extension

- Fill in the outlines and/or shapes using paint applied with brushes, sponges, fabric, spools, bottle caps, plastic forks, or vegetables.

Attention Getters

Materials

- paper plates
- craft sticks or tongue depressors
- scissors
- glue
- markers, crayons, colored pencils or paint
- materials for decorating plates

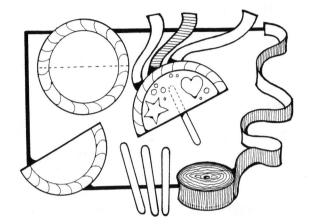

Directions

1. Cut paper plates in half.

2. Glue a craft stick or tongue depressor in the middle of the straight edge of the plate so that two-thirds of the stick projects out from the straight edge.

3. Label the paper plate sign with your name as a room decoration or decorate the plate to represent a special holiday or school project.

Extensions

- Use the paper plate signs and decorations to call attention to a center, an area of the room, or a group activity in which a nonverbal response is required.
- Make streamers from construction paper, art tissue, or newspaper and glue them to the curved portion of the plate. Use the "attention getters" for celebrations or parades.

Crayon Etching

Materials

- heavy paper
- crayons
- paper clip

Directions

1. Using a heavier weight paper for this activity, cover an entire piece of paper with various colors to produce a rainbow effect.

2. Cover the colors completely with black crayon.

3. Etch pictures or designs over the black crayon by scratching the end of an opened paper clip across the black surface.

4. Share your pictures or designs and describe how you made the etchings.

Extensions

- Write a special message along with your crayon etching and present it as a present to a friend, relative, or teacher.
- Write a secret message when you color your paper and have someone uncover the message when the black crayon is scratched off.

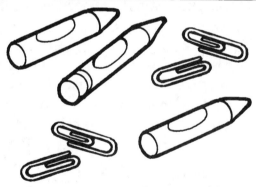

Crayon Rubbing

Materials

- objects from nature
- household objects (towels, crinkled aluminum foil, burlap, window screen, paper/cloth doilies, etc.)
- drawing paper
- crayons

Directions

1. Place one of the objects under drawing paper and color on the paper with crayons. For best results, rub the crayon on its side.

2. Experiment with a variety of objects and/or colors. Make collages of crayon rubbings which convey a theme.

3. Write poems, stories, or songs to go along with the crayon rubbings.

Extensions

- Make a decorative cover for a book you are reading or create your own picture book.
- Make a decorative crayon rubbing frame or letter stencils.

Paint-and-Fold Butterfly

Materials

- construction paper (or plain side of a large grocery bag)
- paint (various colors)
- thinned liquid starch
- newspaper
- paintbrush
- scissors

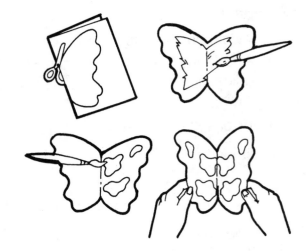

Directions

1. Cover the work area with newspaper.

2. Fold a 9" x 12" (23 cm x 30 cm) or larger piece of construction paper or grocery bag in half widthwise.

3. Keep the paper folded and draw a butterfly wing pattern so that the inner part of the wing is against the fold. Cut out the pattern.

4. Open the pattern and brush liquid starch on the opened butterfly shape.

5. Quickly paint areas of brushed-on or dripped-on paint.

6. Refold and press the wings together. Open the wings and you will see a symmetrical pattern. (*Optional:* Add a body and attach chenille sticks for antennae.)

Extensions

- Write stories, factual information, poems, etc., and attach them to the butterflies. Hang from the ceiling or on a wall.
- Make a colorful, decorative shape book.
- Use glitter, glue, and tissue paper to make mobiles.

Play Dough Possibilities

Materials

- play dough made from recipe on page 12
- newspaper or plastic covering for work surface
- cookie cutters
- plastic knives, spoons, and forks
- paper plates or Styrofoam trays
- *optional:* rolling pins

Directions

1. Prepare the play dough ahead of time. You may wish to make several batches. Use food coloring to color play dough, if desired.

2. Use cookie cutters to make shapes, figures, or structures that relate to themes or topics for holidays or special occasions, etc.

3. You can also roll play dough and form letters to make words or numbers.

Extension

- Make holiday ornaments such as Christmas trees, Valentine's Day hearts, Easter bunnies or eggs, Halloween pumkins, etc.

Class Quilt

Materials

- construction paper (any color), used file folders, or used index paper
- hole punch
- yarn or string
- plastic, blunt-end darning needle
- scissors
- glue
- fabric scraps, wallpaper samples, or construction paper scraps

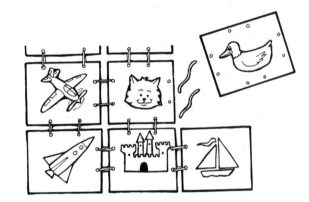

Directions

1. Cut construction paper, file folders, or index paper into 6" (15 cm) squares. Distribute one or more squares to each student.

2. Have children cut fabric scraps, wallpaper samples, or construction paper scraps into geometric or other interesting designs and glue them on the squares.

3. Use a hole punch or scissors to make holes along the edges of the squares.

4. Use the darning needle and yarn or string to sew quilt squares together.

5. Younger children can arrange and glue fabric or wallpaper squares onto butcher paper following a specific pattern, color, or shape sequence.

6. Display the finished quilts.

Extension

- Make a personal quilt that traces your family tree by decorating each with a family member's name and his or her relationship to you.

Seedscapes

Materials

- a variety of seeds
- glue
- butcher paper, construction paper, or index paper
- pencils, markers, or crayons
- scissors
- fabric, paper, or wallpaper scraps
- *optional:* magazines

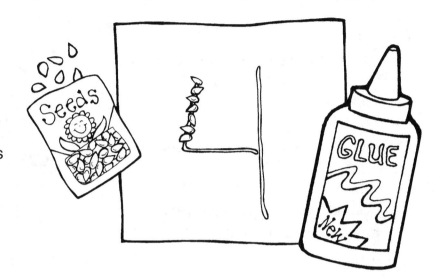

Directions

1. Design a simple picture with markers, crayons, or pencils.

2. Glue a variety of seeds in sections of the picture to create a mosaic effect. For example, if you have drawn a flower in the foreground of the picture, you might glue one type of seed in each of the petals and another type or color of seed on the stem and leaves. (Younger children could make "numberscapes" or "letterscapes" by gluing seeds on number or letter outlines.)

3. If desired, cut out and glue pictures of objects on the paper to show the number or letter that is represented.

Extensions

- On a piece of poster board or tagboard, design a mosaic name plate using a variety of seeds.
- Decorate the outside of a cardboard picture frame cutout by gluing a variety of seeds in all shapes and colors.

Sponge Print Patterns

Materials

- sponges
- tempera paints
- glue
- scissors
- markers
- foil pie tins or Styrofoam trays
- soap, water, and towels for cleanup
- construction paper, butcher paper, newspaper, or computer paper

Directions

1. Cover the work area with newspaper.

2. Pour tempera paint in the trays.

3. On the sponges outline with markers objects or shapes that relate to a holiday, a special event, or a theme. Cut out the objects or shapes.

4. Create sponge prints by pressing sponge cutouts into the paint and stamping the print onto the construction paper.

5. Fill the paper with prints that reflect the holiday, special event, or theme. If several different prints are used on a piece of paper, you may wish to print them in a specific pattern or color arrangement. Allow the paint to dry.

Extension

- Sponge prints made on butcher paper can be used as backgrounds for displaying the children's work. You can use prints to decorate cards, bulletin boards, or as frames for children's writings or illustrations.

Circle of Friends

In this art activity children are encouraged to think about how people become friends. Discuss with others what a friend is. Develop clear, specific examples of how friends should act towards one another. Follow the steps below to prepare hand silhouettes for your circle of friends.

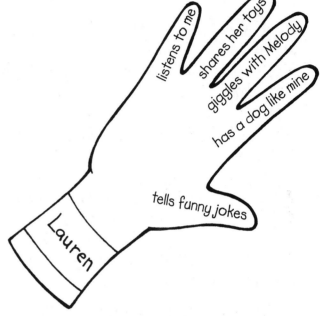

Materials

- construction paper
- pencil
- scissors
- butcher paper
- glue
- markers

Directions

1. Think of ways the person you have selected shows that he or she is a friend to others.

2. On a piece of construction paper, outline your hands with a pencil. Younger children may need assistance with this.

3. Cut out the hand pattern carefully.

4. Draw a wrist band or bracelet on the paper wrist and write the name of the person you selected on it.

5. On each finger, write a way in which your chosen person is a friend. For younger children, have an older partner or a teacher write the children's ideas on the fingers.

6. Make a series of hands for all of your friends. When the hands are completed, join them in a circle (or two, if necessary) by gluing them to a large piece of butcher paper.

Extension

- Make a series of hands which describe famous figures throughout history who were close friends with one another.

Beautiful Bracelets

Materials

- paper towels or toilet paper tubes
- aluminum foil
- macaroni, colored blue (see preparation below)
- white glue
- scissors
- newspaper to cover the work area

Directions

1. Prepare macaroni for this or similar projects by soaking uncooked macaroni in the desired food coloring diluted with water. (Adding a little rubbing alcohol helps the macaroni dry more quickly.)

2. Spread newspaper over the work area.

3. Cut a toilet paper or a paper towel tube along its length. Cut off a section about 2" (5 cm) wide. This will be used for the bracelet.

4. Wrap aluminum foil around the entire bracelet so that the edges close on the inside. Smooth the foil carefully.

5. Glue macaroni around the outside of the bracelet in a decorative pattern.

Extension

- Make a decorative family name plate with aluminum foil and uncooked macaroni and hang it on a wall in a room.

Art and Writing

91

Creatures

Materials

- newspapers
- string or yarn
- scrap materials
- computer paper tear-off edges
- glue
- scissors
- crayons or markers

Directions

1. Roll up a sheet of newspaper to form a creature body.

2. Tie each end with string or yarn.

3. Using scrap materials, glue eyes, ears, mouth, and nose to the center of the newspaper body.

4. Make tentacles by gluing computer paper edges to the creature.

5. Color as desired.

6. Write a story about your creature and share it with others.

Extension

- Hang creatures around the room. Attach riddles, problems, interesting or unusual facts, poems, etc., to them.
- Before rolling the newspaper, place a small gift in the center of the paper. When the creature is completed, write a friend's name on it and give it as a gift. These creatures make great party favors.

Dot Poems

Materials

- glue
- construction paper
- hole punch

Directions

1. Punch holes in a variety of colors of construction paper. Collect the hole punch dots in an envelope.

2. Make dotted frames by gluing the dots around illustrated stories you have written. Display the framed stories.

Extensions

- Make mosaic-like pictures from the dots and write stories or poems about the pictures.

- Use dots to form the letters of your first name. Glue the dot letters vertically on a piece of paper. Write poems or acrostics using the letters of your name.

- Form a series of numbers, as in a zip code or phone number, using the hole punch dots. Glue the numbers vertically on a piece of paper. Write related poems in which the number of words or syllables on a line matches the dotted number.

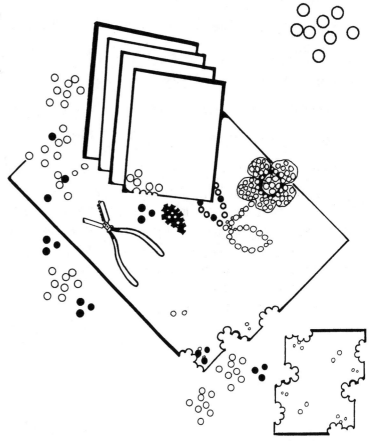

What's in a Name?

Materials

- construction paper or index paper
- glue
- markers
- raw beans, rice, corn, or sunflower seeds

Directions

1. On white construction paper or index paper, use markers to outline your first name. Make large uppercase letters. Younger children may need to have an older partner or adult assist with the letters. Letter stencils are provided on pages 149–153.

2. Put glue inside the outline of the first letter and add beans, rice, corn, or seeds to fill in the letter.

3. Continue adding glue and beans, rice, corn, or seeds until all the letters are covered.

4. Allow the glue to dry overnight.

5. Cut around your name. Glue the name to another piece of color construction paper.

Extension

- Glue dots made from punched-out holes of colorful construction paper inside the outline of the letters or use thick yarn or twine around the outline.
- Fill the inside of the letters of your name with poems or phrases that describe yourself. Use the finished product as a cover for a journal.

Hanger People Self-Portraits

Materials

- hangers
- red, yellow, brown, and/or black yarn (for hair)
- old, long-sleeved shirts
- markers or crayons
- white paper plates
- construction paper
- stapler
- scissors

Directions

1. Draw your face on the bottom of a paper plate.

2. Add hair by gluing yarn to the plate.

3. Place the plate over the hook portion of the hanger.

4. Place a second plate face-up under the hanger and line it up with the top plate.

5. Attach the two plates, with the center of the hanger in between them, by stapling together the perimeters of the plates.

6. Hang the shirt on the hanger.

7. Make hands from construction paper and staple them to the sleeves.

Extension

- Make a hanger person portrait of a friend or family member. Write a poem or special memory that you have of the person and present it as a gift.

Ghost Stories

Materials

- cardboard
- newspaper
- white paper
- scissors
- glue
- markers
- stapler
- pencil or pen

Directions

1. Cover a rectangular piece of cardboard (any size) with newspaper.

2. Using white paper, draw and cut out a large ghost.

3. Glue the ghost in the middle of the newspaper-covered cardboard.

4. Write a story about your ghost.

5. Glue each story to the bottom half of the cardboard.

Extension

- Make a 3-D ghost to attach to the cardboard. Wad up newspaper for a head and use white cloth to cover the head and form the body. Tie white string around the neck while allowing the remaining cloth to drape. Use markers to draw eyes and a mouth on the head of the ghost. Glue or staple the ghost to the cardboard. Add stories or poems.

Triptych Frames

Materials

- glue
- cardboard
- scissors
- ruler
- crayons, paints, or markers
- wallpaper scraps

Directions

1. Measure and cut a 12" x 24" (30 cm x 61 cm) piece of cardboard.

2. Place the cardboard on a work surface. Measure the length of the cardboard and divide it into thirds. Mark the divisions and draw a line to show the thirds.

3. Complete frames by cutting wallpaper into thin strips and gluing the strips all around the edge of the cardboard and along the division lines. (This will make three framed sections.)

4. Write poems to fit inside the middle section of your triptych frame. Next, illustrate the poems and glue the illustrations inside the last section of the triptych frame. Use the first section for a poem title or a photo of the poem's author.

Extension

- Make triptych frames as gifts. Reproduce a famous poem or quote that reflects the qualities of the person who will receive the gift. Glue it in the center section. Write the recipient's name in the first section. Include a personal greeting in the last section.

Honeycomb Heart Cards

Materials

- glue
- honeycomb pads (available at party supply stores and some art supply stores)
- 9" x 12" (23 cm x 30 cm) pieces of pink construction paper or index paper
- red construction paper
- scissors
- markers, crayons, or colored pencils

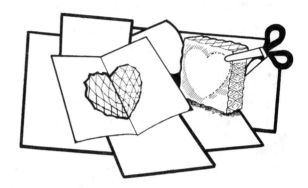

Directions

1. Fold a piece of pink construction paper in half.

2. Use red construction paper to design and cut out a valentine for the front cover of the card. Glue the valentine to the cover and add a valentine greeting.

3. Open the card to the inside. Cut a square of honeycomb paper. (Be sure to cut an appropriately-sized piece to fit in the center of the inside of the card.) Draw an outline of half of a heart along the edge of the honeycomb square. Cut out the pattern.

4. Apply glue to the back and front of the heart half. To glue the heart in the center, place the straight edge of the heart against the fold and close the card. Allow the glue to dry.

5. Write a valentine message on the inside.

Extensions

- Add yarn, ribbon, or confetti made from cut pieces of construction paper to the inside or cover of the card.
- Make cards for other occasions. Match the honeycomb patterns to the occasion.

Sponge Print Haiku

Materials

- sponges
- glue
- scissors
- markers
- soap, water, and towels for cleanup
- tempera paints
- construction paper
- foil or Styrofoam trays
- newspaper

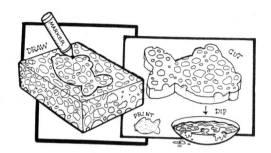

Directions

1. Take a nature walk with your parents or friends and observe the elements of nature. Use your observations to write haiku poetry. Haiku is poetry of seventeen syllables arranged in three lines of 5-7-5 syllables. It may contain direct or indirect references to the seasons or to nature.

2. Prepare sponge print backgrounds. On a sponge, use a marker to outline the object (tree, fish, cloud, etc.) you chose to write about in the haiku poem. Cut out the object.

3. Cover the work area with newspaper.

4. Pour tempera paint in trays and distribute construction paper.

5. Create sponge prints by pressing sponges into the paint and stamping the print onto the construction paper.

6. Fill the paper with prints that reflect the subject of the haiku poem. Allow the paint to dry.

7. Glue your haiku poem to the sponge print backgrounds.

Note: Younger children can make the sponge print backgrounds and dictate information about an object of nature to an older partner or an adult.

Extension

- Make sponge prints for holidays and other special occasions. Use prints to decorate cards, bulletin boards, or frames for displays.

Bubble-Splash Collages

Materials

- various colors of tempera paints
- ¼ cup (60 mL) measuring cup
- ½ gallon (about 2 L) bubble solution
- 6"–12" (15 cm–30 cm) bubble wands (see page 13 for directions)
- white construction paper
- large, plastic container (with lid)
- large, plastic trash bags

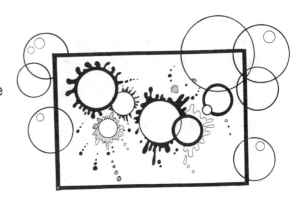

Directions

1. Make arrangements to do this activity outside in an open area.

2. Prepare bubble solution using directions on page 13. Mix ¼ cup (60mL) of desired color paint into bubble solution. (Add more for a darker color.)

3. Place the bubble solution container in a large, plastic trash bag. Blow colored bubbles in the air and try to catch the bubbles on paper.

4. When the bubbles break on the paper, they leave a spectacular array of colored splotches. After you have created your bubble splash art, set the papers in an area to dry.

5. On a wall or large bulletin board, arrange the individual papers in a collage.

Extension

- Have children write about their bubble experience or create poems or stories about bubbles. Display these on the bubble-splash collage.

Shoebox Television

Materials

- shoebox
- two sturdy straws
- 4" x 2½" (10 cm x 6 cm) calculator tape
- craft knife (for adult use only)
- hole punch
- stapler
- crayons, fine-lined markers, or colored pencils

Directions

1. Place the shoebox and lid the lengthwise. Have an adult use the craft knife and cut a 4" x 2½" (10 cm x 6 cm) "screen" in the lid of the shoebox. With the hole punch, make two holes an inch (2.5 cm) past the screen and ½ inch (1.3 cm) from the edge of the box in both the top and bottom of the lid. Make corresponding holes in the box. (It may be helpful to notch the box first with the craft knife and then use the hole punch.) The holes will be used to insert the straws.

2. Think about the story that you want to illustrate and describe. List the main incidents of the story on a sheet of paper.

3. On the role of calculator tape, write and illustrate your story. The first panel should be a title page and the last should say "The End." Write your story at either the top or the bottom of each panel.

4. When the story strip is finished, roll the edge of the title page around one straw while leaving equal parts of the straw on either side. Staple the roll to the straw. Do the same with the other end. Insert the straws into the holes you punched into the box.

5. Put on the lid and your television is done. Rotate the straws to move through the story.

Extension

- Present your television story to friends and family.

My Favorite Book Block

Materials

- ruler
- glue
- crayons, markers, and pens
- tagboard or poster board
- construction paper

Directions

1. Copy the box pattern on page 160 and trace the outline of the unfolded block onto tagboard.

2. Draw the dotted fold lines using a ruler.

3. Be sure to write "glue here" and "bottom flap" to remind you not to write or draw in those three squares.

4. Label one block face with your name, book title, and author.

5. On the remaining five sides, illustrate scenes from your favorite book. Write one or two sentences to describe each scene.

6. Fold the block and glue the sides together and then glue the bottom flap into place.

(Optional: Before gluing the box closed, place some small object related to your book inside the box as a keepsake.)

Extension

- Make a family tree by drawing a picture of each of the members of your family and then write a sentence or two to describe why they mean so much to you and how you are related to them. You can also create a block with drawings of your friends and pets and write a few sentences below each drawing.

Music and Movement

Homemade Musical Instruments

Strike up the band with your own handmade instruments. Follow the directions below and on the following pages to make a tube kazoo, a comb kazoo, a tambourine, a horn, maracas, sand blocks, and a drum. When you and your friends have completed your instruments, gather together and play a few tunes. (See the extensions on page 109 for more ideas.)

Tube Kazoo

Materials

- bathroom tissue tubes
- small piece of waxed paper
- rubber band
- markers, crayons, or paints
- scissors

Directions

1. Cover one end of a toilet paper tube with a 4" (10 cm) square piece of wax paper. Place a rubber band around the waxed paper.

2. Place a rubber band around the tube to hold the waxed paper in place.

3. Punch three holes in a row (about 1" or 2.54 cm apart) lengthwise along the side of the tube.

4. If desired, decorate the tube with markers, paint, or crayons.

5. Try playing some notes on your tube kazoo. Don't be discouraged if you can't make any sounds when you first use it; it takes practice before a sound can be made.

Comb Kazoo

Materials

- hair comb
- rubber band
- waxed paper
- scissors

Directions

1. Cover a comb on both sides with waxed paper.

2. Fasten the waxed paper with a rubber band as shown.

3. Hold the comb to your mouth and hum.

4. Use kazoos for duets, trios, and ensembles. Make up new songs or play familiar tunes.

Tambourine

Materials

- two aluminum pie tins or two paper plates
- hole punch, stapler, or tape
- beans or seeds
- yarn or ribbon
- scissors
- markers, fabric scraps, or construction paper
- glue

Directions

1. Decorate the bottoms of the pie tins or paper plates with paper, fabric, or markers.

2. Put a handful of seeds or beans in one plate. Place the other plate face down on top of the plate with the beans or seeds.

3. The tins or plates can be attached by stapling or taping the rims together or by punching a series of holes around the rim and threading yarn or ribbon through the holes and tying the ends together. Add ribbon streamers if desired.

Horn

Materials

- 30 inches (70 cm) of tubing
- funnel
- colored, plastic tape
- unsharpened pencil
- *optional:* stickers

Directions

1. Use colored plastic tape or stickers to decorate the funnel.

2. Push one end of the tubing into the narrow end of the funnel.

3. Use tape to hold the funnel and tubing together.

4. Make a mouthpiece by placing a piece of tape around the unused end of the tubing.

5. Make one loop in the tubing.

6. Place the pencil inside the loop where the tubing overlaps.

7. Use tape to hold the loop and pencil in place.

8. See if you can make different sounds with your horn. First, press your lips tightly together and blow through the mouthpiece and then slightly relax your lips and blow.

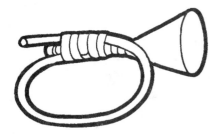  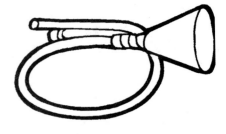

Homemade Musical Instruments (cont.)

Maracas

Materials

- two clean, and dry soda cans
- two unsharpened pencils
- tape
- wallpaper scraps or construction paper
- markers
- glue
- hammer and large nail (for adult use only)
- seeds or pebbles

Directions

1. Put several pebbles or seeds in the soda can. To prevent the pebbles or seeds from spilling out, temporarily place a piece of tape on the open end of the can as you work on the maracas.

2. Have an adult use a hammer and nail to punch a hole in the center of the bottom of each soda can.

3. Push the unsharpened pencil through the bottom hole of the can. Poke the end of the pencil through the hole in the top of the can so that the end of the pencil sticks out no more than $\frac{1}{2}$ inch (1.3 cm).

4. To prevent the ends of the pencil from slipping out of the can, secure them with tape.

5. Decorate your maracas with scraps of wallpaper or construction paper.

Sand Blocks

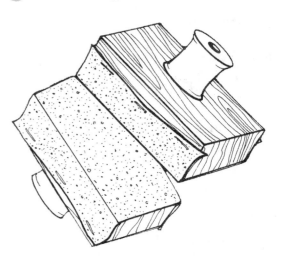

Materials

- two small blocks of wood
  (about 2" x 3" x 1" or 5 cm x 8 cm x 2.5 cm)
- sandpaper
- tacks or staples
- empty thread spools
- wood glue or hammer and nails (An adult should assist when using these materials.)

Directions

1. Measure sandpaper to fit each block so that it almost wraps around the block. Cut the sandpaper to size. Staple or tack the sandpaper to the block as shown.

2. Make handles by gluing or nailing a thread spool to each block.

3. To use the sand blocks, rub them together to the rhythm of the music being played or sung.

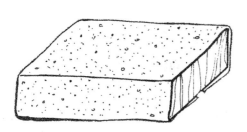

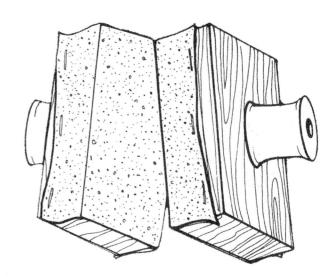

Drums

Materials

- oatmeal box, margarine container, ice cream container, or coffee can (with lids)
- wallpaper scraps, felt scraps, permanent markers, or colorful pieces of construction paper
- glue
- scissors
- string or heavy yarn
- hammer and nail (An adult should assist when using these materials.)
- wooden spoons

Directions

1. To make drums from containers, use them as they are or cover them with decorated paper, wallpaper, or felt. Have an adult punch holes near the top of the container, box, or can. (If using a can for the drum, use a hammer and nail to punch the holes.)

2. To make a strap for carrying the drum, cut a three-foot (one-meter) length of yarn or string and thread it through the holes. Tie the ends together inside the drum. Place the lid on the drum and you are ready to play. Use two wooden spoons for drumsticks.

Extensions

- Add yet another instrument to your band. Fill eight soda bottles with water, one for each note of the musical scale. Gently tap the bottles with a metal spoon and adjust the amount of water in each bottle until you hear the notes of the scale. Practice tapping the bottles in a sequence that will create a tune. Can you invent more instruments?
- Use the instruments to capture the rhythms of some of the your favorite songs. Move to the rhythm of the music as you play your instruments.

Tennis Toss

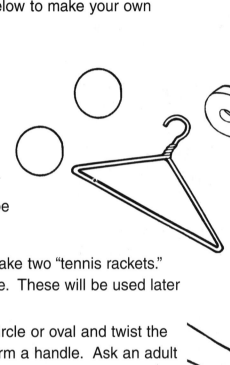

Children will enjoy having tennis matches with their handmade tennis rackets. This makes a great indoor activity on rainy days! Follow the steps below to make your own rackets.

Materials

- old pantyhose
- flexible wire hangers
- metal cutters
- foam balls
- masking tape or electrical tape

Directions

1. Use a pair of pantyhose to make two "tennis rackets." Cut the legs off the pantyhose. These will be used later to "string" the racket.

2. Shape a wire hanger into a circle or oval and twist the ends around each other to form a handle. Ask an adult for assistance if you need to use the metal cutters to reshape or cut the wire hanger.

3. Slip a pantyhose leg over the top of the racket head and tape it firmly at the top of the handle.

4. Wrap the handle with tape and make sure that it is well-cushioned and free of sharp edges.

Extension

- Hold a tennis toss tournament with your friends or family members.

Clothespin Drop

Materials

- coffee can, oatmeal box, or large margarine container
- clothespins

Directions

1. Drop clothespins, one at a time, into a coffee can, oatmeal box, or container. Vary the heights from which you drop the clothespins.

2. Write numbers on the clothespins for you to use as point values. You can then add the number of points earned for successful clothespin drops.

3. You can also play counting games that will help you practice learning your numbers and place values.

Extensions

- Write short words on several clothespins and place them in your container. After mixing them in the container, randomly select several clothespins and try to make short sentences.

- Write different letters on several clothespins and place them in your container. Mix them and randomly select a clothespin. List five words that begin with the letter you selected. Repeat the activity by choosing another letter and thinking of words that begin with the new letter you selected.

Parachute Pop-Outs

Materials

- two parachutes, each made from a large sheet measuring about 8 feet (2.4 meters) in diameter
- 20 rubber or foam balls, about 2" (5 cm) in diameter (Children can bring these from home.)

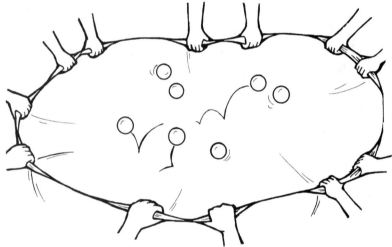

Directions

1. Divide the children into two groups. Place them evenly around each parachute.

2. Have the children grip the parachute around the edges.

3. For a warm-up activity, have the groups shake the parachute vigorously.

4. To play the game, place 10 balls on each parachute. After the start signal has been given, have the groups shake the parachutes and attempt to pop the balls out of it. The first team to shake the parachute until all the balls bounce off and onto the ground wins the game.

Note to the parent: You can substitute chalk erasers, ping-pong balls, or other soft, nonbreakable items for the rubber balls. The number of items placed in the parachutes can also vary.

Extension

- Hold a timed Parachutes Pop-Outs competition to see which team can pop out the most balls.
- Practice your math skills by counting how many balls each team was able to pop out during the competition.

Balloon Volleyball

Materials

- yarn or string
- inflated balloon
- long table or two desks
- two chairs

Directions

1. Use yarn or string to make a "net" by attaching the yarn to the tops of two chairs that have been placed with their backs against the ends of a table (or two desks put together).

   If a rug area or outside play area is preferred, set up a volleyball "net" with the yarn by extending it between two tall chairs or poles.

2. Balloon volleyball is an informal game in which you and your friends try to hit an inflated balloon back and forth across the yarn. For variation, use two balloons at a time.

3. Points are scored by a team when the opposing team fails to return the balloon.

4. The balloon can be volleyed as many times as necessary in order to return it over the yarn.

5. To make the game more challenging, allow a specified number of volleys before the balloons must be returned.

Extension

- Play balloon volleyball with different shaped balloons.

Dramatic Play

Read the Classics

The importance of reading to children cannot be stressed enough. The following experiences enhance the reading process. Seeing words in print, relating speaking to the reading process, and exposure to different experiences, new vocabulary, idioms, grammar, punctuation—these are but some of the benefits to be gained through shared reading. The full scope of such benefits—social, emotional, and intellectual—is perhaps unlimited.

Materials

- Use appropriate versions of classic fairy tales, such as *Three Little Pigs, Cinderella, Beauty and the Beast, Goldilocks and the Three Bears, The Twelve Dancing Princesses, Jack and the Beanstalk,* and *The Little Red Hen.*

Directions

Choose a classic fairy tale. Select the activities appropriate for the participants.

- Show the cover of the storybook at hand. Ask a child to tell something about the picture. Any response will do. One child may be familiar with the story and want to relate a part of it.

- Do some phonics activities. Introduce characters that begin with the letter sounds you wish to teach or reinforce such as Beauty for the letter B or Jack for J. If you are using flash cards associate the written word with the oral language.

- Use a choral speaking technique by asking children to join in repetitive phrases that are used in fairy tales. For example, the wolf in The Three Little Pigs says, "I'll huff and I'll puff and I'll blow your house down." Each time he says this, have children repeat this along with you. You may wish to copy the phrase onto chart paper so children can follow along.

- Make simple character masks or name tags. While wearing these, have children retell the story. Masks can be made by using half a paper plate with holes cut for the eyes. Let children decorate them to represent the characters they are acting out. Punch a hole on either side of the mask. Attach yarn and then have children put them on. Name tags can be made by writing the name of the character on a piece of construction paper, punching holes on the sides of it, and tying yarn through. Hang the tags around the children's necks.

- Write captions from the story on blank paper. Duplicate and have children create their own drawings to correlate with the caption.

Read the Classics (cont.)

Directions (cont.)

- Give each child a piece of 12" x 18" (30 cm x 46 cm) drawing paper. Ask children to draw their favorite part of the story. Younger children can dictate the meaning of their picture as the teacher writes the words at the bottom of the drawing while older children can write their own. Everyone then views their classmates' pictures and attempts to put them in the correct sequence. Gather the pictures together in book form, punch out holes on the left side, string yarn through the holes and create a book.

- Choose characters from a book and make flash cards with simple pictures of characters on one card and their names on another set. Have children match the two. They can do this in small groups or individually.

- Make little books. Write the text for younger children. Older children may copy the text from a chart of the little book that you create. Have them assemble and staple the books. They may draw pictures to illustrate the story.

- Many classic fairy tales have much in common. Among these common elements are:

  a. The beginning is "Once upon a time . . ."

  b. Magic events or characters are part of the story.

  c. One of the characters is someone of royalty.

  d. One of the characters is evil or wicked.

  e. Animals are often characters.

  f. Special numbers, such as three and seven, are contained in the story.

  g. Often there is a message or a lesson involved.

  h. The ending often reads ". . . and they lived happily ever after."

  Help children identify common elements in fairy stories. Make a chart and have the children help fill it in. They may use the information to create stories of their own.

- Put on a short play by using hand puppets (socks or paper bags) or stick puppets. Re-enact a favorite scene from the selected fairy tale.

- Play Fairy Tale Concentration. Draw characters from various fairy tales on a set of cards and make another set of cards with the characters' names. Turn them over and mix them up. See how many cards you and your friends can match.

- Make a bookmark with a drawing of your favorite fairy tale character and give it to a friend or family member as a gift.

Pencil and Paper Games

Clothespin Punctuation

Materials

- clasp clothespins
- fine point marker
- sentence strips

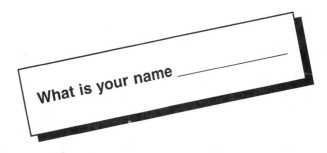

What is your name _____

Directions

1. Using sentence strip paper, write simple sentences omitting the end punctuation. On the back of the strip, write the proper punctuation.

2. On the clothespins write the punctuation marks required to finish the sentences.

3. Give the children the sentence strips and the clothespin. Let them clip the proper clothespin to the end of the sentence. Children may turn over the sentence strips to check their own answers.

Pencil Scrabble

Materials

- grid with 1" (2.54 cm) squares
- pencils

Directions

1. Divide into groups of two to four children. Give each group a grid and pencils.

2. In the middle of the grid, write a long word such as "elephant." Children then build words using the letters that are already on the grid. The letters must form a word with an already existing word. The letters may not touch any other letter unless it also forms a word.

3. Scoring may be one point for each letter or one point for each vowel and two points for each consonant. You may wish to use specific word categories such as parts of speech or theme or topic-related words.

Pencil and Paper Games (cont.)

Alphabetico

Materials

- markers or pencils
- index cards

Directions

1. For each group of players, make a set of identical index cards. On each index card write one word with which children are familiar. These may be spelling, vocabulary, or theme-related words.

2. Put children into small, equal-size groups. Each group chooses a leader who is given the set of cards.

3. After the start signal is given, the group works as quickly as possible to alphabetize the cards. They may lay their cards on the floor or a table.

4. When a team is finished, the leader raises his or her hand. Check to see if the order is correct. The team to finish first with the correct order is the winner.

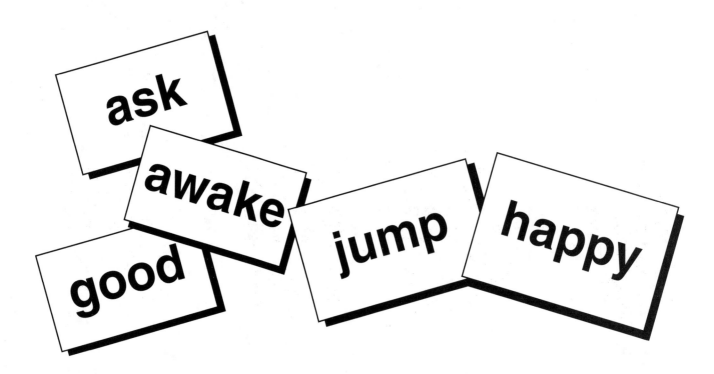

Dramatic Play

There is a great deal to be derived from dramatic play. Children are able to express themselves socially and emotionally while acquiring important social skills which they will use throughout their lives. They are learning about other people and varying points of view. During these experiences, children also acquire language in a natural setting. They engage in oral language to its fullest and gain a better understanding of the way people think and act.

Imagination is the key to creativity. Allow children to explore their world through activities which encourage imagination. Find new uses for familiar items, pose "what if . . ." questions to encourage creativity, and provide ample time for children to brainstorm new ideas in a comfortable environment.

The activities on pages 120–125 will help you and your children to prepare and present puppet shows and explore other avenues of dramatic play.

Sock Puppets

Puppets are excellent for use in dramatic play. They allow children the opportunity to express themselves through a different medium. This is especially helpful for children who are self-conscious about expressing themselves orally.

Encourage children to make a variety of puppets. Develop and present a play using the puppets as characters. The play can be simple or elaborate, depending on the children's interests and abilities.

Materials

- old socks
- assorted pieces of fabric or felt
- felt, yarn, string, sequins, or buttons
- scissors
- fabric glue

Directions

1. Children can create faces by cutting out and gluing shapes onto the sock.

2. Use fabric scraps or ribbon, yarn, string, sequins, and/or buttons to decorate the puppets.

Clothespin Puppets

Materials

- clothespins
- scissors
- yarn
- markers or paints
- scrap material, lace, rickrack
- construction or index paper
- craft glue

Directions

1. Have children create their own puppets by making faces on the clothespins using markers or paints.

2. Glue hair and clothing to the clothespins using scrap materials, construction paper, etc.

3. Clasp clothespins can be made into face puppets by decorating one outside surface with a face and the other with a mouth. Open and close the clasp clothespin to make the puppet's mouth move.

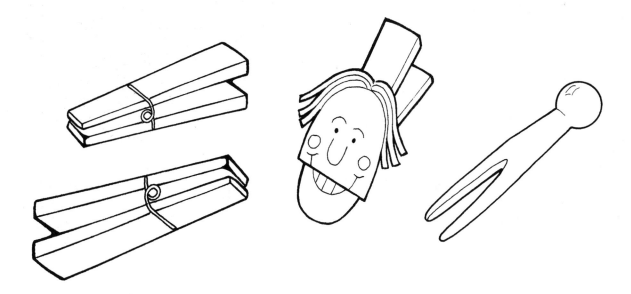

Stick Puppets

Materials

- paper plates
- craft sticks or tongue depressors
- stapler
- crayons or markers
- yarn
- construction paper scraps
- craft glue
- optional: fabric scraps, buttons, beads, sequins, etc., to decorate puppets

Directions

1. Create characters by drawing faces onto paper plates using crayons or markers.

2. Use crayons or markers to outline facial features.

3. Use construction paper scraps or yarn to make hair. Add decorative materials to make the puppet more unique.

4. Staple craft sticks or tongue depressors to the plates to create puppets.

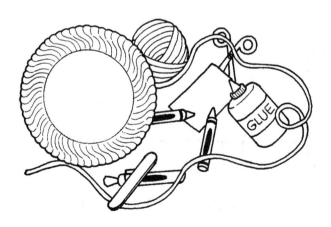

Puppet Stages

Use puppet stages with puppets that children have made. Directions for three different types of stages are provided below.

Materials

(See individual activities below.)

Directions

Table Stage: Hang an old sheet over a low table. The puppeteers kneel on the floor behind the table. The puppets move on top of the table.

Box Stage: Have an adult use scissors or a craft knife to cut a large square hole in the top half of a large appliance box. The puppeteers sit or kneel inside the box. The puppets move in the square hole.

Sheet Stage: Hang a rope or heavy string across a corner of the room about two feet (61 cm) from the floor. Drop a sheet over the rope. The puppeteer kneels behind the sheet in the corner. The puppets move above the sheet.

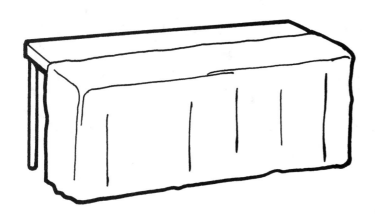

Dragon Parade

Materials

- several yardsticks or dowels 36" (1 m) in length
- several 18" (.5 m) circles cut from cardboard
- markers or tempera paints of various colors
- masking tape
- hole punch
- thick yarn
- *optional:* material scraps, buttons, glitter, ribbons, etc., to decorate circles

Directions

1. Decorate the 18" (.5 m) circles with different designs and materials. On one of the circles, draw the head of the dragon. On another circle draw the tail of the dragon and add some yarn at the end as its tail.

2. Tape a yardstick or dowel to the back of each circle.

3. Punch holes on each side of the circles that will make up the body of the dragon. Punch a hole on only one side of the head and tail circles. Cut pieces of string to connect the various parts of the dragon.

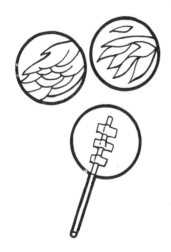

Charades

Materials

- slips of paper
- pencil
- box

Directions

1. Before beginning this activity, determine what words or situations you wish to act out. These may be a current topic of interest, types of words such as antonyms or synonyms, or something related to a theme.

2. Write the words on slips of paper.

3. Fold and place them in a box.

4. Divide into small groups. Let each group select a slip.

5. Have each group pantomime their selection to the other groups.

Extension

- As you become more familiar with this game, act charades out individually.

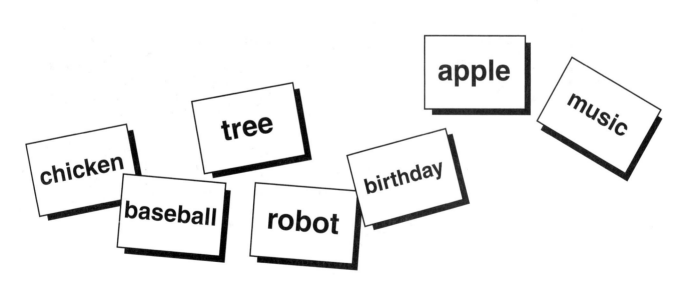

Number Fun

Math Games

Toss to Numbers

Materials

- old white or light-colored sheet
- markers
- several beanbags

Directions

1. Draw 10 geometric shapes on a sheet.

2. Randomly place a number from 0–9 on each shape.

3. Have children toss a given number of beanbags on the numbered shapes.

4. Add the numbers displayed on the shapes or have children call out the names of the shapes that have beanbags in them.

Extension

- Have children use the beanbag toss to reinforce multiplication facts. Use larger numbers inside the shapes for more complicated computations.

Toothpick Towers

Materials

- toothpicks
- white glue or miniature marshmallows
- paper plates

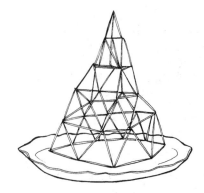

Directions

1. In groups or individually, build towers using toothpicks. The structures should be as strong as possible.

2. Attach toothpicks with white glue or connect them with marshmallows. Encourage children to use as many geometric shapes as possible in designing their towers.

3. Identify and count the number of triangles, rectangles, squares, angles, sides, etc.

Extension

- Create toothpick animals or buildings with toothpicks and marshmallows. Identify as many triangles, rectangles, squares, angles, sides, etc., as you can.

Pickup Sticks

Materials

- scissors
- craft sticks
- markers
- paper or plastic cups
- construction paper or index paper

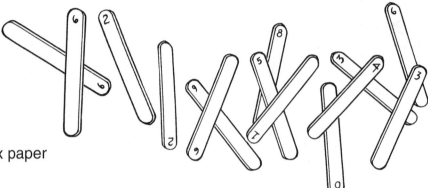

Directions

1. Write numbers 0 through 9 on the ends of craft sticks. Make several sets of 0 through 9 numbers so that a group of children can participate at the same time.

2. Place each set of 0 through 9 craft sticks in its own cup.

3. Cut 3" (8 cm) square math cards from construction paper or index paper. Use these to write math facts that can be matched with the numbers on the sticks. For example, a card with 3 x ____ = 6 would be matched with the stick displaying a 2 since the number 2 would complete the equation on the card. Math facts and information provided on the cards can be changed for children to practice math.

4. To play, have children place the numbered sticks into the cup, shake the cup, and toss the sticks out by turning the cup upside down. The child then picks up a math card from the cards that have been placed face down. When the child solves the problem on the math card, he or she picks up the matching numbered stick or sticks from the pile. (**Note:** Younger children can match the number on the stick to the number or matching dots on a card.)

Extension

- Create more difficult games as basic games become too easy.
- Make up a game for a math concept that needs reinforcement.

Computer Paper Edge Math

Materials

- dot matrix computer printer paper (Form-feed computer paper edges can be used for a variety of activities. If possible, obtain a variety of colors.)
- construction paper
- glue

Directions

1. Tear the edges from the computer paper. Store the edge strips in a large box until you are ready to use them.

2. Use the holes in the computer paper edges for counting activities. Count by 5's, 10's, etc.

3. Tear the edges into groups of five holes and use as manipulatives for practicing multiplication facts for Do the same for any of the basic multiplication facts.

Extensions

- Since the holes in standard dot matrix computer printer computer paper are 1/2 inch (1.3 cm) apart, the paper edges can be used for standard measurement activities involving U.S. customary measurement. Younger children can also measure objects and make size comparisons using the paper edges as a non-standard measuring tool.

- To practice addition and subtraction, have children tear computer paper edges randomly and add or subtract the number of holes represented by the torn sections.

- Have children display their knowledge of addition, subtraction, or multiplication facts by gluing computer paper edges on a piece of construction paper to represent the facts.

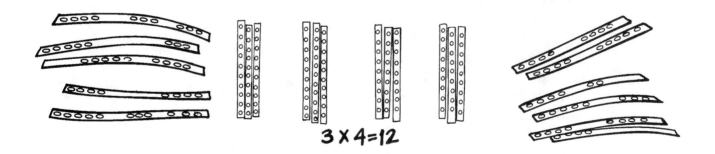

$3 \times 4 = 12$

Can of Beans

Materials

- dried lima beans
- coffee cans
- tape
- permanent markers

Directions

1. Tape around the rim of the coffee can to prevent injury from metal edges.

2. Write a number on each lima bean. Use as many or as few beans as you wish.

Extension

Children can practice one or more of the following activities:

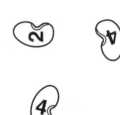

- With eyes closed, take a bean from the can and determine if it represents an odd or even number.

- Remove several beans from the can, add them up, and determine if the sum represents an odd or even number.

- Take two beans from the can and decide which represents the greater number.

- Shake the can and dispense several beans. Place them in order from the least to the greatest value or from the greatest to the least value.

- Choose several numbered beans from the can and estimate the sum of all the numbers represented on the selected beans.

130

Time for Math

Materials

- white paper plates
- paper fasteners
- markers
- crayons
- scissors
- hole punch
- index cards

Directions

1. With scissors, punch a small hole in the center of the paper plate.

2. From another paper plate, make an outline of a minute hand and an hour hand. Be sure that the clock hands are in proportion to the clock face. Color and cut out the clock hands.

3. Punch a hole in the end of each clock hand in order to fasten it to the center of the clock.

4. Mark off the hours by adding the numbers 1–12 around the rim of the plate in the appropriate places. Older children may wish to add lines for minute intervals along the rim of the clock face.

5. Use a paper fastener to attach the clock hands to the center of the clock face.

Extensions

- Write a variety of times on index cards. Randomly draw cards and move the clock hands to represent the time written on the index card.
- Prepare a deck of index cards with problems involving time. Adapt the index card information to meet the needs and abilities of the children.

It's in the Bag

Materials

- poker chips (red, white, and blue); craft sticks; or scraps of red, white, and blue construction paper
- paper lunch sacks
- chart paper
- crayons or markers

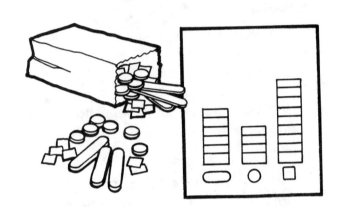

Directions

This activity is designed to provide hands-on experience with ratio, proportion, and probability.

1. If you choose to use construction paper, cut the various colors into equal-sized squares. If craft sticks are to be used, color a tip of each with one of the three color choices.

2. Divide into small groups. Provide each group with a paper lunch sack containing a random assortment of colored chips, paper squares, or craft sticks.

3. Have each group make columns on charts to represent each color. Randomly draw a square, chip, or craft stick from the bag.

4. On the chart, mark with a tally the color that was drawn from the bag. Put the items back in the bag. Draw and tally again. Do this a total of 10 times.

5. Add up the total number of red, white, and blue tallies in each column.

6. Compare each group's results. Discuss the responses in terms of probability. Repeat the activity a few times and compare the results. The teacher could also prepare a large chart of all group results and average the red, white, and blue columns. Discuss the results.

Extension

- Experiment with different proportions of red, white, and blue items and predict the outcome of their random draws.

Living Graphs

Materials

- masking tape
- paper
- pencils, crayons, markers, etc.

Directions

1. Use the masking tape to form a large graph on the floor. The "living graph" is formed when the children are used to fill in the rows of the graph. Make a list of questions to ask children and have them line up on the graph behind their responses.

2. Record the information and discuss, for example, which row had the most people or how many more people chose row A than B. Have children make a paper and pencil copy of the graph using the responses from the living graph.

Extension

- Choose from among the following additional questions or use topics that coincide with a theme or subject being studied.

  —Do you have a pet?

  —How many people are in your family?

  —What is your favorite color?

  —What is your favorite school subject?

Do You Have a Pet?

Place Value Cakes

Materials

- several empty toilet paper tubes
- glue or tape
- scissors
- red and yellow construction paper cut into 2" x 3" (5 cm x 8 cm) rectangles
- pencils, crayons, or tempera paints of various colors
- three large, shallow rectangular boxes or large shoeboxes

Directions

1. Color or paint the empty tubes.

2. Draw and cut the red and yellow construction paper into flame shapes. Make the red flames a little larger than the yellow flames.

3. Glue the red flames to the inside of the tubes.

4. Decorate each rectangular box or large shoebox with color pencils, crayons, and/or paints.

5. Label the first box as the "ones" box, the second as the "tens" box, and the third as the "hundreds" box.

6. Tape the bottoms of several candles on each box and discover the fun of learning about place values.

Extensions

- Have children make decorative box "cakes" to help celebrate the birthday of a friend or family member.
- Have a child make a birthday box "cake" with a lid to preserve keepsakes of his or her birthdays.
- For celebrating the 100th Day of School, divide the class into groups and make 10 cakes, each with 10 candles on top. Display the cakes at a 100th Day Celebration.

"In the Doghouse" Math

Materials

- small, clean milk cartons
- craft sticks
- glue
- crayons or markers
- construction paper

Directions

1. Cut off the top portion of the milk carton and glue construction paper to cover the remaining sides.

2. Decorate your milk cartons to look like doghouses. Label the front of one carton with an addition sign, another with a subtraction sign, and the remaining carton with the words "Pet Number Sticks."

3. Turn your craft sticks into dogs or cats and number each stick from 0–10 at the bottom.

4. Use the craft sticks to practice addition and subtraction by using the numbers written on the bottom of the sticks.

Extension

- Introduce the concepts of nouns, verbs, and adjectives by labeling three milk cartons with these categories. On craft sticks write examples of nouns, verbs, and adjectives and place them in a decorated milk carton. Mix up the craft sticks and match the words on the sticks with the correct category.

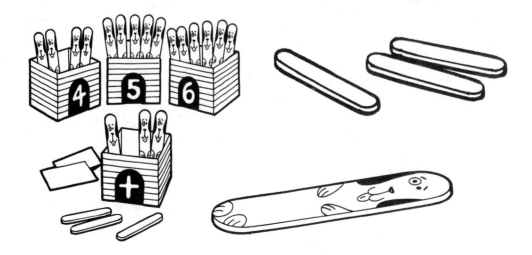

Sensational Science

Garden Science

Eggshell Wonders

Materials

- eggshell halves
- grass seed
- potting soil
- markers
- egg cartons
- water

Directions

1. Use markers to draw faces on the shell halves. Place the eggshell halves in empty egg cartons.

2. Fill the shells about two-thirds full with soil.

3. Sprinkle some grass seed in each shell and add water. You will really enjoy watching your eggshell sprout grass.

Spongy Garden

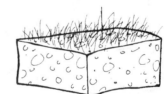

Materials

- sponge
- needle and thread
- craft stick
- birdseed or grass seed
- clean spray bottle
- water

Directions

1. Thread a needle. Tie the end of the thread to the middle of a craft stick.

2. Push the needle and thread through the center of the sponge so that the craft stick rests at the edge of the sponge. This will prevent the thread from slipping through the sponge.

3. Sprinkle the upper surface of the sponge with seeds. Hang the sponge garden in a sunny window and spray with water daily. Watch grass grow!

Sink or Float?

Materials

- feathers
- cork
- string
- piece of plastic
- seeds
- money
- beans

- buttons
- pine cones
- tongue depressors
- tub of water
- construction paper

Directions

1. Under the supervision of an adult, begin lowering items into a tub of water one at a time.

2. Discuss with the person who is helping you with this activity what seems to be happening.

3. Make a chart on a piece of construction paper with the title "Things That Float Versus Things That Sink." Objects or pictures of objects may be glued on the chart or drawn by children. You can also surround your chart with prediction cards listing other objects you think would sink or float.

Feed the Birds

Materials

- small or large milk cartons
- string or yarn
- craft knife or scissors
- hole punch
- bird seed or animal food
- *optional:* tempera paint

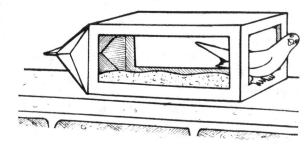

Directions

Make one of the following types of bird feeders. Observe the activity of the birds daily. Discuss regional birds, bird habitats, and other information that relates birds to a study of animals.

Ground Feeder: Rinse out an empty milk carton and allow it to dry. Cut out three "windows," two from opposite sides of the carton and one from the bottom end of the carton. Paint the carton if desired and allow it to dry. Place the carton on its side as shown. Fill the feeder with birdseed and place it outdoors on the ground, in a tree, or on a wall ledge.

Hanging Feeder: Rinse out an empty carton and allow it to dry. Cut out four "windows," one on each side of the carton with a craft knife or scissors. Be sure an adult supervises or performs this task. Paint the carton if desired. Allow it to dry thoroughly. Punch two holes in the top of the carton and tie string to the holes as shown. Fill the bottom with bird seed or animal food and hang the feeder in a tree or by a window for observation.

Fun with Smells

Materials

- fresh lemon or orange
- chocolate cookie
- vinegar
- peanut butter
- cinnamon
- peppermint flavoring or candy
- Styrofoam or plastic containers with attached lids from fast-food restaurants

Directions

1. Place each item in a separate container and close the lid.

2. Poke a few holes in the lid.

3. Smell each container and decide what is in it by using the sense of smell.

4. Encourage older children to find out how the sense of smell functions. Younger children can write about or relate stories about their favorite smells.

Extensions

- Encourage children to recycle Styrofoam or plastic containers from fast-food restaurants. Have them keep a chart of the recycled items collected in one month.

- Use the containers for storing art, math, and science supplies. Label each container for easy identification.

Weighing and Measuring

Materials

- large plastic tubs
- uncooked oatmeal or rice
- containers of various sizes and shapes
- large spoon or scoop
- plastic measuring cups
- water

Directions

1. Fill containers with rice or oatmeal. Compare the amount of rice or oatmeal required to fill each container.

2. Predict which containers will hold more, less, or the same amount of rice or oatmeal.

3. Weigh the filled containers on a balance scale and compare the weights of the various containers.

Extension

- Children can replace the rice and oatmeal with water and try these and other weight and measurement activities.

Sand Timer

Materials

- two large jars
- construction paper
- fine sand
- watch or clock with a sweep second hand

Directions

1. Make a funnel from construction paper. Place the funnel in the top of one of the jars.

2. Pour sand into the funnel-shaped paper for a specified time (one minute, two minutes, three minutes, etc.). Use a watch or clock to time the pouring of the sand.

3. When the specified time has been reached, stop pouring the sand. The sand that was poured represents the amount of time you wish to measure when using the sand timer. Save it in the jar.

4. To use the sand timer, simply place the funnel in the second jar and pour the sand into the funnel. When all the sand has fallen into the second jar, the specified time has been reached.

Extension

- Use the sand timer for timing various activities throughout the day.

Balance Scale

Materials

- two thin pieces of wood, each about three feet (one meter) long (Two soft-wood yardsticks or meter sticks work well.)
- pushpin
- two paper clips
- thin string
- scissors
- two plastic or paper cups or two foil tart tins
- empty coffee can
- sand, dirt, or clay

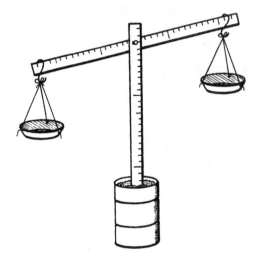

Directions

1. Mark the exact center of one of the pieces of wood.

2. Place one end of the second piece of wood perpendicular to the first piece at the point where the center mark was made.

3. Press the pushpin through both pieces of wood so that the first piece of wood is attached but still able to move freely without wobbling.

4. Hold the free end of the second piece of wood in the center of the coffee can and fill the can with dirt, sand, or clay. The can will serve to anchor the scale.

5. Open both paper clips so that they each form a letter "S."

6. Hook a paper clip near each end of the movable piece of wood.

7. Attach three equal lengths of string to the free end of each paper clip.

8. Poke three equidistant holes in each of the two cups or tins and attach one of the strings to each hole.

9. Balance the scale by adjusting the position of the paper clips or add a small piece of clay to the balance arm to level it.

When the Wind Blows

Children can measure wind direction with this easy-to-make wind vane. Have children make wind vanes and use them while learning about weather.

Materials

- long nail
- permanent marker
- pencil
- empty thread spool
- tape
- plastic drinking straw

- scissors
- 6" (15 cm) square piece of thick cardboard
- 8½" x 4" (22 cm x 10 cm) piece of tagboard
- small piece of clay

Directions

1. On tagboard, copy an outline of an arrow. Make it about 6" (15 cm) long. Cut it out and tape the center of the arrow to one end of a straw.

2. Carefully push the nail through the center of the cardboard square until most of the nail shows above the cardboard.

3. Place a small piece of clay over the small portion of the nail that is still exposed under the cardboard. Flatten the clay by pressing the cardboard gently onto a tabletop. Be sure to get adult supervision for this step.

4. With a marker, write the four wind directions on the square cardboard in the correct order.

5. Place the spool over the nail. Slip the straw and vane through the spool opening. The straws should turn easily.

6. Place the wind vane outside and make observations. It may be necessary to anchor the base of the wind vane. (Note: Be sure that the north marking on the cardboard is facing north!)

Extension

- Have children observe wind direction daily. Keep a record and discuss observations.

Homemade Binoculars

Materials

- toilet paper tubes
- glue
- string or yarn
- hole punch
- *optional:* tempera paint, markers, or stickers

Directions

1. To make one pair of binoculars, paint or decorate two toilet paper tubes if desired. Allow them to dry thoroughly.

2. Glue the tubes together to form binoculars.

3. Punch a hole on the outside edge of each tube.

4. Attach an 18" (46 cm) piece of string or yarn to the holes to form a strap to wear around the neck.

Extension

- Have each child make his or her own binoculars. Enjoy an "I Spy" science hunt on a fair-weather day at a park or on a field trip. After your trip illustrate, discuss, and/or write about what you observed through your homemade binoculars.

Quick-and-Easy Magnifier

Materials

- tagboard or cardboard
- eye dropper
- craft stick or scissors
- clear tape
- water
- magnifier pattern (below)

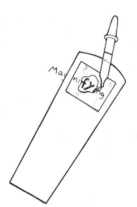

Directions

1. Reproduce the magnifier pattern onto a piece of tagboard or cardboard.

2. Cut out the magnifying glass outline. Cut out the inside square to form a window.

3. Cover the square area with a small piece of clear plastic wrap. Use clear tape to secure the plastic wrap in place past the edges of the square.

4. Place a few drops of water from an eye dropper into the magnifying window.

5. Hold the magnifying glass horizontally over the objects that you are observing.

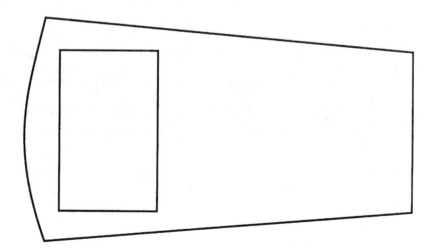

Tornado!

Materials

- two clear plastic 2 liter-bottles
- duct tape
- scissors
- water
- pencil
- paper towel
- ruler

Directions

1. Fill one bottle half full of water.

2. Cut a strip of duct tape about 1 inch (2.5 cm) by 2 inches (5 cm).

3. Cover the mouth of the bottle that contains the water.

4. Poke a hole in the tape with a pencil. Enlarge it slightly.

5. Put the mouths of the bottles together with the empty bottle on top. Tape the mouths together at the necks.

6. Flip the bottles so that the bottle with the water is on top.

7. Hold the bottles by the necks and quickly swirl them in circles parallel to the floor.

8. Set the bottles on the table with the empty one on the bottom. Watch the water swirl in a funnel shape as it pours into the empty bottle. It looks like a tornado!

Patterns and More

148

Letter and Number Stencils

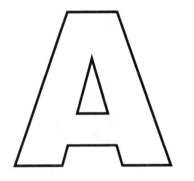

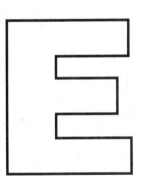
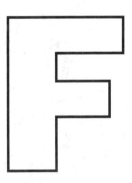

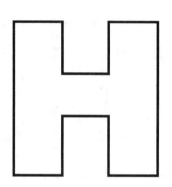
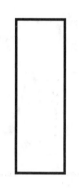

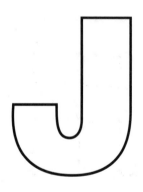
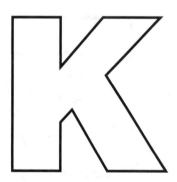
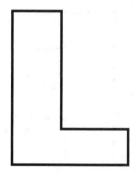

 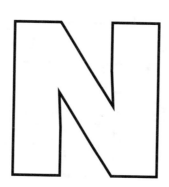 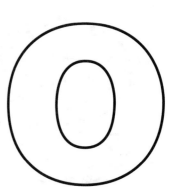

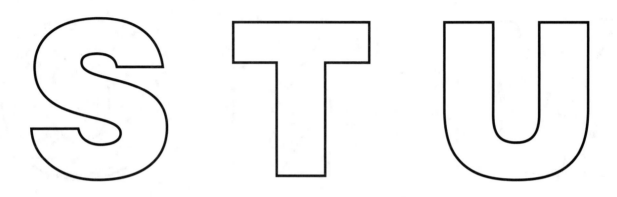

Y Z O

1 2 3

4 5 6

7 8 9

154

Clip Art

Use the patterns below and on pages 156–158 to decorate a variety of projects from this book.

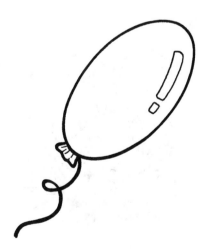

Reproduce the pattern below onto construction paper or tagboard. Cut it out. Decorate the door knob hanger using crayons, markers, paper scraps, etc. Cut out the marked circle along the dashed line. Hang on a door knob.

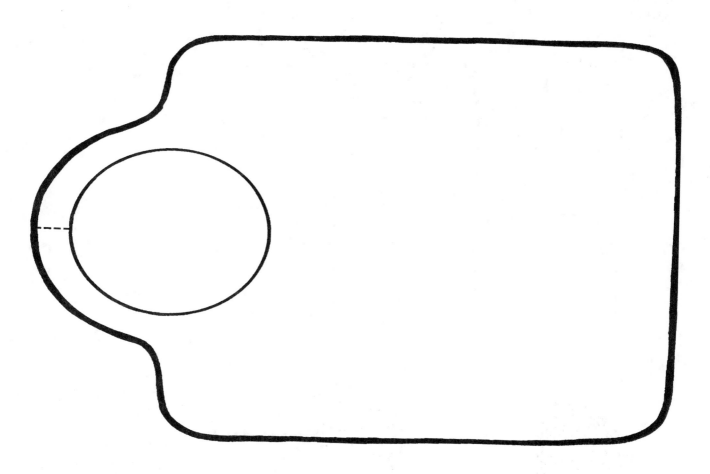

Box Pattern

Reproduce the pattern below on index paper or construction paper. Cut out the pattern along the solid lines.

Fold along the dashed lines and glue the tabs in place to form the box. Allow the glue to dry. Have children decorate the box with designs, written messages, or theme-related illustrations. Tape string or yarn to one side of the box and hang it for display. **Note:** Enlarge the pattern as needed.

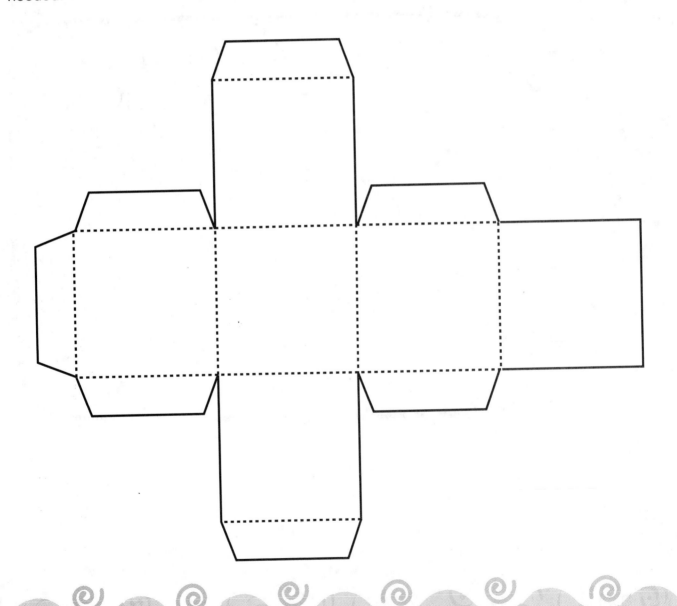